Easy, Cozy, Frugal Homemak

How to Stay Home on a Tiny Budget

By Mrs. Kate Singh

Author of The Frugal Life and A Sweet Life In Homemaking

Find Mrs. Kate Singh on YouTube: Coffee With Kate

Edited by Perla Thornwood

Cover by Kate Singh

Copyright © 2021 by Kate Singh
All rights reserved. This book or any portion thereof may not be reproduced or used in any manner whatsoever without the express written permission of the publisher except for the use of brief quotations in a book review.

Table of Contents

Chapter 1　Home Sweet Home

Chapter 2　Planning, Saving, and Homesteading

Chapter 3　Cleaning, Organizing, and Decorating an Old House

Chapter 4　Stocking the Pantry, and Frugal, Tasty Recipes

Chapter 5　Learning Frugality from the Professionals

Chapter 6　If You Are Super Poor

Chapter 1

Home Sweet Home

I am going about my nighttime routine.

I set my teapot to brew and put my little sausage dog outside one last time to do her business so that she will sleep through the night without waking mummy. The automatic back porch light goes off too soon, and she stands out in the dark yard barking into the darkness at whatever might be out there waiting to snatch her up. Sometimes, when I feel generous in motherly spirit, I will go out onto the steps, encouraging her, and stand guard while she makes it happen.

I go about turning off Christmas lights inside and outside. I pull thick curtains closed, both for privacy and to keep in the warmth. Our house was built 120 years ago—a time before adequate insulation. We use very efficient space heaters in each room that we are spending time in. This way, I do not have to continually run the central gas heat and run up the bill.

We stay up late during the holidays and watch movies from Disney Plus, a gift subscription we received from a friend. I am in heaven. I have tortured all of us with *The Sound of Music* and *Mary Poppins*, all the old classics.

It doesn't matter too much when we go to bed, since it's holiday time and we are on break from schooling. I am a homemaker with homeschooled children. We live a delightful life in so many ways, including the choice to have late nights and being able to sleep in now and then. We can play as much as we like; we are free from the confines of rigid schedules, alarm clocks, commutes, public schools, and the workplace.

I am full of gratitude for this. However, my husband goes out into the world to work and deal with the good, bad, and the ugly in order for me to be able to stay home.

To show my appreciation, I work hard to keep my place in our home. I clean and scrub the house plenty, but I also decorate it to the utmost charm for almost no money. If I want to buy something for the house, I sell something else in order to have the cash for the desired item.

I cook so much. I bake often. I wisely stretch each paycheck to keep building up our lives and home. I study canning, gardening, and food preservation. I keep learning more ways to clean better, save more, master frugality, and the conservation of our resources.

I have earned this position through self-education and practice, making many, many mistakes along the way. I was not raised to be a housewife. I worked hard as a child, having many responsibilities since I was the only child of a single mother. It was just her and I, so we did everything to get by. But my mother did not teach me how to clean thoroughly or well. She did not teach me to cook at all since she loved that job. I did not learn how to do laundry properly and, although I worked in the garden, I did not know how to grow a garden, just how to weed and water. And money, oh Lord, my mother was not the best with money. We sometimes had plenty and then, whoosh! It was gone, and we would struggle for the rest of the year. She was terrible at managing the household finances.

So, we do not all have that mother, grandmother, or aunt who guides and teaches us all the skills to run a home and raise a family. Some of us must learn on our own.

My teachers were stacks of library books and lots of YouTube channels. That is how I learned gardening, cleaning, cooking, canning, and preserving. I listen to wise women and men who know how to live on an extraordinarily small amount of money.

Times are changing rapidly right now. In the last decade, we have had a large recession, government shutdowns, and now, due to this pandemic, quarantines. Unemployment rates are up. The number of families on government assistance is growing and food banks are overwhelmed.

What will the future bring? Will it be another Great Depression? A recession far deeper and sadder than the one from just 13 years ago?

Or what if we begin a new green economy in earnest? There is an enormous new economy in sustainability, recycling, veganism, green energy, and much more. But will the government dive into it fearlessly?

Until then, we must rely on ourselves and practice our sustainability. We must start our green path and go back in time to recover some of our grandparents' or great-grandparents' traditional homemaking and homesteading ways.

> *"He who fails to plan is planning to fail."-Winston Churchill*

I do not listen to the fear talk, but I do prepare for natural and unnatural disasters. I enjoy organizing; it has become a sort of hobby. I stock the pantry, find ways to be more frugal, and find most items we need or want for free. We can do many things to save money, make life more comfortable, and be less dependent on the government and others. That is our mission.

We have not always been so smart. I have been in debt and spent a small inheritance on nothing in just two years. We purchased things that we wanted, not needed. When we had our first child, we bought hundreds of things we never used. We purchased new furniture for the whole house, only for it to break later. Some of it aged poorly, and most of it I just detested quickly. I have grown to love thrift store furniture.

I did not save well in our early years and often found us overdrawn by the end of the month. We paid everything and had grocery money, but there was always a shortage of funds. It was my lack of shrewdness.

But over time, I have learned all the tricks. Paying yourself first is the biggest trick we used that transformed our life, quite literally. You can live on much less than you think. That was another lesson, or trick if you will. Hearing these things and putting the ideas into action is another.

Downsizing is another thing that helped us to live below our means. Downsizing can look different for everyone. For us, it meant buying a HUD home that required work. It meant purchasing the ugly house in a small town because the mortgage (including insurance and property taxes) would be less than any rent we had ever paid. It meant taking care of old cars. It meant less stuff because we lived in a small, affordable house. It meant doing less costly activities and finding free things to do and have.

I will share our humble life, hoping that it inspires you or at least takes the fear out of making a lifestyle change. We are imperfect and have failed many times to get to this place. This way of life is not for everyone; I get that. I have adjusted my vision to fit this budget. I tend to like the frugal, happy life.

Take what you like and leave the rest.

Chapter 2

Planning, Saving, and Homesteading

When you think of homesteading, you may envision milking goats, making cheese, a flock of hens in the yard, and vast fields of vegetables. We don't do all that. We bake bread by hand, hang the laundry on a line outside, maybe can some triple berry jam. We did try hens at first, and I do not know that we will do it again. They are far more work than it appears.

We chose a big yard with our new home, and it gives us room to take on chickens, rabbits, and even a goat if times get hard. I am hoping they never do go to this extreme. I do not have the stomach for raising animals, especially not for butchering.

Last summer we moved to a new house in a new gardening zone. The soil was different; the climate was different. We used a small tiller at first, then we got smart and rented a big tiller to dig up our new garden.

Our garden is 1,200 sq. ft. We added horse manure from a new farm, but the waste had wood chips, and it drained nutrients from the soil instead of enriching it. We did not have enough compost in our first season. The garden was a flop.

There was some confusion with the seedlings, and I wound up with 20 squash plants and little else. The greens did great. So, we ate huge pans of sautéed greens and plenty of pans of sautéed squash and onions. Later we enjoyed a few tomatoes. The melon never fulfilled its destiny.

A couple of years back, a book was introduced to me titled *We Had Everything But Money: Priceless Memories of the Great Depression* by Deb Mulvey. Photos and memoirs of those who grew up during the Great Depression era filled the book. The memoirs were *not* of the heartbreaking and tragic side of that time, thankfully. My soul could not take that. Instead, the stories were of parents and grandparents who persevered with grit and creativity to overcome hard times.

Almost every story had a few common themes. One of those was hard work and the willingness to take on any job for any amount of money. Another was having fruit trees and huge vegetable gardens in their backyards. Some had chickens as well, and these were the city and town dwellers. Most farmers could get by well as they had plenty of food since they had what they called truck gardens, the mothers' kitchen gardens, cows, pigs, and chickens. The other common theme was lots of love, faith, staying positive, helping family, friends, neighbors, and not letting their children know that they were going through hard times. Back then, it was far easier to hide the hard times because everyone had them.

Then we have the other "ingredients" that most of us know from that time: making do with what you have and taking care of what you have.

Today we throw things away when they break or tear. We get things for cheap at dollar stores or Walmarts. We want more and more. We want better, faster, and more sparkly. We are brainwashed by commercials and advertising, bombarded with visions of a "better life." We see such lovely homes, cars, clothes, and things in those commercials, movies, even in sitcoms. I am always surprised at how nice the houses are in movies about people struggling financially.

There is not much reality these days. If you watch a movie from the '70s or even '80s compared with today, it is shocking. People used to look real, and now they are beyond perfect. Everyone drove an old beater car, and now everyone has a new car. Homes have doubled in size, maybe even double and a half.

How do we afford it all? Credit, loans, and more credit. But we pay the price later. It can tick along simply fine until the market has a downturn, a job is lost, or a partner gets injured or becomes seriously ill.

I like to have a plan. I have plans A and B; sometimes C. Lately, we live between B and C. We pay only for essentials, and if there is any money left over, it goes into our savings.

Lately, I have been reading many Depression era books, and I just received some books by Daisy Luther. She is a traveler and a prepper. She has been flat broke while raising her daughters by herself. She has a book called the *Ultimate Guide To Frugal Living* as well as some prepping and canning books that teach how to stock your pantry for a year within three months. I am fascinated with this woman and am eager to learn all that I can from her. I also recently read an excellent book I would highly recommend called *Eviction: Poverty and Profit in the American City* by Mathew Desmund.

We are not flat broke, and I would not want to call that into our existence. Why do I read all these books about the Depression and frugality? Why, oh, why do I read this stuff? Am I morbidly fascinated with poverty? Do I fear poverty?

No and no.

We are not middle class but we are not far from the government poverty line either. I would say we are blue-collar working folks. We must work a little extra to make it all work, but we are comfortable.

Tonight, as I write this, my husband is snoring away and my children are tucked in asleep. The dogs are also tucked in and snoring. I am tucked into my big chair in the living room with the heater directly on me. I have a candle glowing, so I do not have the lamp on to wake up the house. I hear the rain coming down outside. We are incredibly fortunate. We have a home with no leaks in the roof, electricity to turn this heater on, warm, soft beds, and plenty of food to feed us all.

That is what the books do for me. History teaches me what can happen with the market, the workforce, and the housing industry. It gives me compassion and enables me to reach out to others and show by example that there is another way to live during these modern times, and that it does not have to be piled high with sacrifices and cheap living.

We do not earn that much money, but we live so comfortably. We have built a nest of comfort and all that is good, but with limited funds.

We aren't as dialed in as some frugal families that have fully paid for homes and are retired by the time they're in their 30s. We are the little group off to the side: we aren't frugal heroes but are practicing the craft and reaping some of the harvest.

My husband and I started late in life. We married late and became parents late. I am now 50 years old; my husband is a bit younger. We are raising two boys, ages 6 and 8. We own two properties, and neither one is paid for in full.

But I am pleased with and surprised by our progress. We started with nothing, and in the nine years since we got married, we have two healthy children, three healthy dogs, and two old homes that we have scrubbed, painted, and breathed new life into. I never thought that we would be landlords, much less have a family of our own. I truly saw us renting forever; but I kept dreaming, we kept saving, and I kept harassing loan officers to see if we could make things happen. We had issues: too small of a savings account, no credit/bad credit, and low wage jobs. It took years to straighten things out.

We finally made things happen when I surrendered and started looking for a cheap home in a small town, even though it was not in our ideal location. We were outbid many times before we made an offer on a house that was not even our last choice, but became our only choice.

That house became our home for three years, and we made it so charming that we grew to love it deeply. Our street was somewhat fixed up, and the town is now up and coming.

But this was not the full dream I had envisioned for our family. No, I had found our dream town up in the mountains. It called to me. The problem was that it was far, far out of our price range. The area I wanted to move my family to was a place most people would say, "It's so beautiful there, but much too expensive!"

I made dream boards and filled my wish box with little folded up pieces of paper inked with desires. "Dear God, it's me, Kate." But by the third year, I remembered the verse, "Faith without works is dead." Hmmm. I got to work. We got to work. My husband Bali was initially not on board, but then he started working part-time in that little mountain town. I cannot, for the life of me, remember how that happened. But he started working in a charming market in a forested neighborhood, and he was impressed with the locals. He said they were unlike most people he had ever met. Polite, friendly, well-mannered, and cheerful! I said, "Of course, look at where they live! Who wouldn't be cheerful living there?"

Once a week, I took the boys to an Earth school up there. I joined the local co-op where I did my grocery and organic bulk food shopping. I was making friends. The boys were making friends. We practically lived there. But we had no savings, only a wish.

In the third year, I woke up to reality. I started writing books and filming for my YouTube channel like crazy. My husband began a part-time job, and then he took every extra shift available at his main job. We got lucky when two employees went to India for a few months and he worked all their shifts. It was not fun, but we packed away some money then. My channel grew and my books were selling well.

Then I began practicing everything I had ever read, written, watched, and learned about being frugal.

We grew a big vegetable garden and ate from it through the fall. I have to say we ate more eggplant than I would ever wish upon anyone. I canned 20 jars of spaghetti sauce from a tomato patch I planted in the front yard. We had stuffed many fruit trees in the yard, but it takes years to get fruit. Fortunately, the neighbors' nectarine tree grew half of itself over our fence and blessed us every summer. On the other side, another neighbor had a huge lemon tree that also grew half on our side of the fence, and we enjoyed a lot of lemonade.

I began baking and cooking from scratch like it was a newfound religion, and we did every free thing that we could. We walked everywhere to save on gas, and we frequented parks for fun. We stayed home and read, listened to music, watched TV, played, gardened, made art, wrote books, and so on.

We learned how to enjoy - *really enjoy* being home and staying busy with hobbies and projects. My eldest son is an avid reader and an incredible artist. My youngest was obsessed with Godzilla, so there was lots of building of Tokyos and acting out monsters' invasions (he is now obsessed with The Titanic). We loved free movies on VUDU. We loved the library. We would borrow one or two bags full of books every few weeks. Some libraries are even giving patrons a receipt that shows them just how much they are saving by ordering library books instead of buying them. We have saved ourselves somewhere in the tens of thousands over the years.

We stripped the budget down to nothing, and even gave up our fantastic health club where we spent summer evenings swimming after Bali would come home from work. We had no cable, but we had an antenna on the roof, and I loved all the sitcoms I got from the public channels. I have many fond memories of sitting on my bed folding piles of laundry while watching *According to Jim* or old sitcoms from my childhood like *Night Court*.

I loved that time. I loved that home. It kept us cozy and safe and cradled us as we worked hard towards another goal. We were able to live on as little as $1,600 per month. That may sound like a lot, but in California, it is a miracle for a family of four.

Finding the house we are in now was insane. We went through so many deals. A mobile home on two acres fell through, and another place was in such bad shape that the realtor asked us to do some work on it so that it would pass inspection (we did, like fools, before we finally threw in the towel and cut our losses). Then there was a straw bale house that became a short sale. After three weeks, the bank decided not to sell it to us. We even looked at living in a gated community but that simply is not us. With our gardens and clotheslines, we would have been asked to leave within weeks.

But there was a house that kept showing up. It disappeared for a bit but reappeared later. It had been a pending sale, but it did not work out, apparently. It was the last house left and it was not even within our budget. I negotiated a price that made my realtor cringe, but she played her role and put in the offer. The offer was declined. I offered a little more. The next morning I felt moved to force the seller's hand. I called my realtor and asked that the seller give me an answer that day so we could proceed or move on. You see, we had been working on finding our house for almost a year. You must detach emotionally when finding your future home. It is all business until you have the keys in hand.

It worked. The seller agreed and signed that day. Lucky for us because the next day, he received a cash offer for the original asking price! Holy Toledo! We had been outbid and outshined on everything for months, so this was a rare victory. Poor people do come out on top sometimes!

I look at prices in this area now and about half of the homes I look at are going for almost double what we paid. We made it just in time before more housing market insanity befell us all.

This house was no beauty. It had unattended land for God knows how long, the seller painted the house a strange pastel army green, and it had industrial carpet on the floors. Outside, the house was painted a light tan. There was even a token rotten rodent in the water closet. I kept pointing the smell out, but my husband said it was my imaginings until he tore the cupboard out. I tell you, perimenopause gives you a heightened sense of smell.

Today the house looks as though a family of wild, shabby chic hippies moved in. We brought all our cheerful colors of paint with us from the old home. We even brought some of our fruit trees; we dug them right up and hauled them up the hill. Our compost! Crazy people that we are. Leave nothing behind. My ratty little greenhouse got pelted in the first hail storm up here and now has many "air" holes in the top.

We tore out the carpet hoping to find old wood flooring and we did. Unfortunately, there were a million nail holes that had ruined it. We also found padding, foam, linoleum, and pressboard. It was a mess. We were able to purchase bamboo flooring on deep clearance and it turned out to be even cheaper than faux wood or laminate.

We hired a handyman team to do the big, challenging jobs. Their work was lacking, but they got the worst of it accomplished. They tore out all the layers of the old floor and installed the new floor. They painted the interior of the house all white to cover that asylum green.

The white walls did not have the brightening effect I thought they would. They gave off a strange gloom. I went to the tiny shed and pulled out paints and started mixing. I started with the kitchen, and as I coated the walls with a butter yellow, the joy inside began to grow. I had not bonded with the house until I started painting. From there, Bali got into it, and we mixed and painted every day. When we started running out, we found more paint that friends did not want. We even found paint that had been stored and forgotten in the shop where Bali worked. We painted like crazy for weeks until every room was a different color. Some colors turned out amazing despite the odd mixing. One color turned out strange and risky but it worked in the end.

Bali fixed and tightened the floors after I spent months cursing the gaps that were significant enough to allow one too many Legos to be wedged in. After the floors were fixed, I loved them so much that I gave away most of the area rugs.

We spent all spring and summer working. We had two enormous dead trees removed from the front yard. That was a huge mess and it left us cleaning, raking, sawing, and stacking for weeks. Because of the pandemic and empty store shelves, we decided to plant a huge garden right away. We put up a fence and tried tilling with various ineffective tillers until we finally hauled home a rental tiller that dragged Bali back and forth over the 1,200 sq. ft. garden. I ran off to Green Acres Nursery & Supply and brought home a truckload of fruit trees and berry bushes. I bought piles of seeds.

We planted an orchard immediately. Our orchard has a variety of different trees: three cherry, three apple, one apricot, one lemon, one mandarin, one pomegranate, and two pluot plum (I'm not a plum person, but I love pluots). We also planted a hybrid pear tree and my beloved nectarine tree that we brought from the other house. We also have two blueberry bushes.

There are two ancient plum trees on the property from the old days, along with a pear tree that needed some severe pruning, some blackberries along the fences, and a fig tree. The yard looked so bare, but as spring unfolded, we found these trees as well as berries and wild onions, dandelion greens, pink roses, peonies, and the neighbors' English walnut.

As we planted seeds in cans that I'd saved from our holiday feast, stacked wood, and pruned the trees, I thought about what we would have done if we arrived with no extra funds. There is so much we could have done without the money. We had the wild greens and onions. With some pruning and care of the old trees, we did harvest many pears that summer. We ate many plums and could have made jam if I was a plum jam type of person. We had plenty of wood for a stove but decided against it. The solar company paid to remove the enormous, dead black walnut tree that towered over the house. There was another big tree in front of the black walnut that was also dead. I made a cash deal with the tree guys for that tree's removal as well.

We could have lived with the floors, and all the paint we used was free. I think it was a wasteful mistake painting the whole house white. We rushed things and wasted money. If you slow down, oftentimes it becomes clear that not so much needs to be done and you can find plenty of free things, such as free cans of paint that others might have in their garages just collecting dust.

There is a lot you can do for truly little. Paint and plants do wonders for the interior of a house. Outside you can have a no-dig garden, which would have been smart since we are dealing with clay soil. Many people suggested it, but I had this notion that we needed to plow the earth.

This winter, I smarted up with that garden. It went right back to rock hard, and we made the mistake of layering horse manure loaded with wood chips. That soaks up the nitrogen, as I was informed later.

So, last fall, we hauled in manure from a previous farm we'd used that did miracles on our old garden. It is aged and free from wood chips.

After watching a female Zen monk from Korea on *Chef's Table*, a show on Netflix, I was so influenced by her garden that I decided right then and there to change the way we would garden in the future. Jeong Kwan and her wild garden made an impact. She just let it do its thing, trusting nature.

We hauled in our trusted and aged manure from the old farm. I threw my compost right out there on the ground, and when the leaves started falling, I rejoiced as they covered my garden. I also planted a cover crop of wheat-rye. I read that it is excellent for clay earth and returning nitrogen and nutrients to the soil.

We learned so much from both homes. Both times we worked too hard, did too much, and spent more money than necessary. I thought we had wisened up with the first house, but we made new mistakes with the second house. We are masters at learning through mistakes.

But we are older now and taking the easy road. We will have a no-dig garden. We will probably not do much more work to this house for years to come.

Chapter 3

Cleaning, Organizing, and Decorating an Old House

This house leans this way and that. If you roll a marble, it will let you know how the room is angled. All the rooms are a hodgepodge of wood paneling or plaster. The ceilings are either wood or floating pressboard. The sink counter is a swirly, sparkly '70s design. The tub is cheap plastic - not even properly sealed. The kitchen is dark until about 2 p.m. The laundry room is always cold. The linoleum throughout the kitchen, bathroom, and laundry is an ugly brown.

And yet, I adore this house. It took time and work. Many women talk about finding their dream home, and it is love at first sight. They move in, and all is lovely. Although I felt drawn to the house immediately, I did not feel this. The large porch drew my attention. I closed my eyes and could picture many delightful summers of having meals with friends and neighbors at a charming long table that I would set up right on that porch. I could almost smell and taste all the cups of coffee that I would sip while sitting on the steps as the sun rose, watching the warm morning unfold. I was drawn to the enormous yard because I could see all the fruit trees and garden vegetables we would plant, anxiously waiting until we could enjoy our delicious harvest.

Then there was the charming old town that we could walk to and all the trails and forests for us to explore, also within walking distance. I was in heaven. We could walk to stores, libraries, trails, and all that was important to us. I love living in town for that very reason. I feel like I have Plan C in place when we can get to things on foot. And whatever we cannot walk to, we can take a bus to. There is a bus that stops on our street several times a day.

Three seasons have passed, and our home is now cozy and charming.

My sink had a wall over it. I used to say a kitchen window was non-negotiable, but sometimes you count your losses and move onward. Following the advice from the wonderful community on my YouTube channel, I put up a big mirror over the sink, and lo and behold, it was a *brilliant* decorating move. It reflects so much light and opens the room right up.

Christmas arrived, and while going through boxes of ornaments, we found a twinkle lights net for the bushes outside. I was playing around and hung it on my kitchen curtain rod. I was pleasantly surprised to see that it gives it a magical warm glow.

We need lamps, but we have decided to put up those warm string lights in the living room, kitchen, and bedrooms. To some, this is tacky. To me, it is delightful. The only thing that matters is what you think of your home, not others. *You* live in it, after all.

When it comes to paint, like I mentioned in the previous chapter, we went with lots of color for each room. Dark blues, shell blues, odd blues, butter yellows, flower yellows, Mediterranean pink, pastel lime green, toasted orange. It all works.

Then there's the furniture. The load I brought to the house was not working. It was great in my little '40s stucco, but in this old house with small, square rooms, it was overwhelming, large, awkward, and chunky.

I had no money to work with, and we did not want to dump our furniture. I tried to work with all of it for months and finally decided that, as Marie Kondo, author of *The Life-Changing Magic of Tidying Up: The Japanese Art of Decluttering and Organizing* would say, "It wasn't sparking joy." It was sparking resentment. I began giving it away. I scrubbed and bleached the L-shaped three-piece couch set and found one lucky fellow who took it all away. I cleaned each piece and gave each one a new family. As our house emptied, I searched and found more free furniture than I ever dreamed of. And it all looks fabulous in this house!

I did buy a couple of pieces, but I could sell some of our things to afford them. One was a very plump pillow couch in light brown that had spent its days in a guest cabin unused—scored for $125. The other piece was a small kitchen hutch for $50. Then there were small things like rag rugs and baskets I use in the pantry—all part of my country theme. I believe I spent less than $250 to redo my house completely. Oh, and then there is a king-sized bed frame that we found inexpensively at a thrift store. It did not quite fit and was missing a few pieces, but Bali sawed, hammered, and added pieces until it was perfect for the shape of our mattress.

Cleaning

As I get older, I find more creative interests such as walking through the forest with my dog and boys for hours, writing books, creating vlogs for YouTube, deepening relationships with friends, and getting to know my neighbors. I also have mild scoliosis and now due to age, lower back issues - fun stuff like that. I cannot work like a dog all the time, keeping my house lovely and clean. However, I love having a clean, tidy home. I feel grounded, peaceful, and motivated when my home is fresh and put in order. It is pure mental well-being.

Cleaning is also therapeutic, as many will agree. If you have an issue that you cannot resolve or work through all that well, you do a deep house cleaning on Saturday, and after a few hours, you feel good about life again, with the added bonus that now your house looks sparkly.

I am big into decluttering, I just do not understand how we still have so much. I read Marie Kondo's first book back before she became a household name. I have been downsizing and decluttering since before it became a trend. I have been putting bags and boxes out on the street with FREE signs for years. I enjoy giving things away and creating space in my home.

I have watched *Minimalism: A Documentary About the Important Things* on Netflix, and there is now a second documentary from the same producers called *The Minimalists: Less Is Now*. I just watched it this morning on the first day of 2021. I thought it might inspire me to simplify more, even though I'm not a hoarder or a big shopper. I am also not going to be a true-blue minimalist. I am somewhere in the middle, maybe more of a hygge type.

I used to have schedules. I would fill up the monthly calendar with certain days to do certain chores. For example, Monday is wash day, Tuesday is cleaning day, Wednesday is baking day. Then time moves on, and you wind up baking on Monday and cleaning on Saturday because every week something changes and it's difficult to stick to the routine.

I watch cleaning videos on YouTube, and the only ones that impact me are the ones where the house looks like a bomb hit, and then they clean the whole place up on a time-lapse. Love those! I drink my homemade latte with an extra shot of espresso, watch the wild mess be put right in just 20 minutes, and am ready to clean. Most cleaning videos are the same. The homemaker runs the vacuum back and forth, does some dishwashing, picks up toys. I want to learn new tricks to clean like a pro. I want my house to glimmer in the sunlight through the window, not just show all the streaks and dust I missed.

There is a cleaning channel on YouTube called *Gypsy xo*. I watched this housewife and her mother clean in a few videos, and I was never the same again. My house cleaning has been transformed. Most gypsy wives are immensely proud homemakers. I learned this from a documentary long ago when I became fascinated by this culture. Gypsy wives take enormous pride in their homes, be it a mobile home, RV, or stick house. They keep it scrubbed clean and do it all while taking care of their families. This motivates and inspires me.

I clean in such a different way now. One day a week, I work hard, maybe for six hours, and I still do not get it all done. I think that if I could commit to a few hours a day everyday like the housewives of old, my house would sing my glorious praises.

I now pull out couches, stoves, and shelves, cleaning under, behind, and in the back. I sweep under beds, wash walls, bleach doorknobs and light switches, wipe down couches and cushions, shampoo my area rug, and wash the throw rugs often. I dust, and I have chosen to use the broom and hand sweep the whole house twice a week. The vacuum is for a quicky every other day. I do sweep the kitchen daily. When I clean the toilets, I clean from top to bottom. Once a week I take the bidet apart to clean it thoroughly. I have boys. Need I say more? The porch gets swept and tidied, stairs and back stoop swept daily.

I wash out and organize the refrigerator and freezer more frequently. I clean out the oven monthly. I was never consistent about these things before.

I have been a housewife for almost ten years now, and I am still learning, still honing those skills by learning to clean deeper, cook better, and be wiser with the money. It is a process, a journey with many pitfalls - one of them being boredom and domestic drudgery.

But you can avoid these two nemeses. It happens, but it happens with any job or career. You hit the wall. The best thing to do is step back, take a break, rest, and have some fun. Then assess what is making this job so hard, tiring, or dull.

I love keeping a home. But some days I am tired shortly after the day has begun; usually when the house has been neglected, and is a mess. Waking up to a wrecked kitchen is a real emotional drain in the morning when all you want to do is brew some coffee and sit in a scrubbed clean kitchen to make your daily list.

Having too much stuff or trying to do too much is another weight. I have learned to clear things off my schedule and clear out clutter from my home to make it easier to maintain and make sure I have plenty of time at home. I love being at home.

I used to love to run around. I would drive here and there, never wanting to be home, but I learned to enjoy being home over time. I surrendered, and now I have hundreds of projects I love to do right here. I do not think my children have uttered the words, "I'm bored." We have hobbies that we become immersed in. I create a sweet ambiance with cleaning, scents, candles, good cooking, freshly-baked bread, and music. I have coffee brewing daily and maybe a good movie on TV in the afternoon. We have rituals of taking care of our pets, our home, ourselves, and having special times in the day. We gift ourselves for the hard work.

I get re-inspired from books and YouTube channels when necessary. I work out on my elliptical and watch videos for a good half hour and then get to work.

My Cleaning Process

First I clean the kitchen. I wash dishes first, then counters, large table, and then scrub the stove, which is often a mess from all the daily cooking we do. Once the kitchen is clean, I whip up a quick lunch of chili, homemade pizza, or macaroni and cheese with vegetables. I keep it simple on cleaning days.

Next, I vacuum the area rugs in the living room and the boys' room. The other carpets get a good shaking outside over the porch railing before I hang them out in the fresh air. If it's time to wash them all (a monthly task), then I load them in the washer with detergent and a little bleach.

I roll up the area rugs in the living room and boys' room and put them up. I then hand sweep the whole house, starting from the front, going clockwise to the back laundry room. I then take my cloth mop and rinse the cloth strip in hot water to prepare it. I use a spray bottle with water and cleaner. Sometimes I use Fabuloso, Mr. Clean with a fresh scent, or vinegar with a squirt of Dawn. I mop all the bamboo floors. In the kitchen, bathroom, and laundry room, we have old linoleum. I use a steam mop and spray bottle of water and cleaner to clean all those floors. Sometimes I add a little bleach to clean the floors, but please be careful if you decide to try it. Many cleaners and bleach do not mix well and can cause illness or even death. When I had babies on the floor all the time, I just used vinegar and dish soap. Even animals can get sick, so I try to stay natural but sometimes I feel the floors need a deep cleaning.

As I am cleaning floors, I am washing rugs and dog blankets. The dogs have beds, but I found that covering them with thick blankets and just washing those was so much easier than disassembling beds and cleaning the covers.

I dust all the furniture.

In the bathroom, I scour the sink, counter, and toilet bowl with Ajax. For the tub/shower, I will either use a shower cleaner or Ajax. I will sometimes use a shower cleaner instead, depending on how dirty it is. The rest of the bathroom is cleaned with a bathroom bleach cleaner and old towels. I usually use gloves for this chore.

On another day, I will wash the bed linens and clean windows and mirrors. I will admit that I can put off windows for months. I don't know why!

With the global pandemic, I got in the habit of taking a cloth and bleach spray and wiping down light switches, phones, computers, and doorknobs.

Once a month, I go through the house and do a little purging. I put it all in a box or bag if it is clothing. We take it to the thrift store, or I put it on the street with a FREE sign.

I am only buying rare books for my library, such as those from Mrs. Sharon White and Daisy Luther, and Depression era memoirs.

I go through the kids' clothes each season and give away decent pieces that no longer fit or will not fit by next year when we would bring them out again. I store winter andsummer clothes in a bin in the closet until it's time to pull them out. When I bring out the season's clothes, I go through them as I put them in drawers. Some will be bagged up for Goodwill or the local thrift store.

When our clothes get too ragged to wear or give away, I cut them up for rags to clean.

Sustainable and Frugal Cleaning

All of my cleaning tools are washable and reusable. I do not buy paper towels, except for once in a great, great while. I just bought a pack of paper towels the other day. I would have purchased just a roll, but for some reason, they only had packs. It has been a year since we had any, and these will last for, literally, years. I use rags for everything. I use kitchen towels for kitchen work and cloth napkins for our meals and snacks.

I use a broom for most of my floor cleaning. I use a vacuum that has washable filters and a canister; no vacuum bag. I use a steam mop and a Bona mop with a thick cloth that attaches with Velcro to the bottom of the mop handle and floor piece. I use a spray bottle, or I save old cleaning bottles to reuse.

The cheapest cleaners are the homemade ones with vinegar and dish soap, or scrubs with baking soda and lemon. You do not need to buy anything other than that. As previously mentioned, I do like to keep bleach on hand, and I still use Ajax. It was something I grew up with, what can I say? Fabuloso is cheap, and a jug lasts years and years.

The best value for your money when it comes to laundry soap is Roma or Foca, powdered detergent you can find at Latino stores. I do not know how well they do in an HE washer, but some say it works fine. They are great for the other washers and hand washing. I buy Surf soap from Sam's Club. It is a massive box for dirt cheap and works well, even in the HE washer we have.

If you are ever in a bind and have no laundry soap, the quickest and cheapest to make some is using this recipe from Mary Hunt's blog *www.everydaycheapskate.com*: https://www.everydaycheapskate.com/quick-n-easy-homemade-laundry-detergent-update-with-tutorial/

Note: If you don't have washing soda, you can just spread baking soda on a cookie sheet and bake for one hour at 400 degrees Fahrenheit.

Hygge and Minimalism

Minimalism is the word on the street, and I think it is beautiful and imperative for a new culture springing up from the ashes of 70 plus years of consumerism. What we've been doing as a society is not sustainable nor is it good for our beloved Mother Earth.

We acquire all our goods used and repurposed from Goodwill, various local hospice and thrift stores, and the free section on Craigslist. I have given away furniture and/or belongings we no longer use or want. Everything was recycled. I love nothing more than purging and downsizing. My house of 1,100 sq. ft. is even too much for me at times. I like to make open space.

I am hygge through and through. I love my shelves of books that I refer to often and reread. I love scented candles and paintings that make me smile when I look at them. I love to have colorful pillows tossed on our overstuffed couch and my overstuffed chair with a small quilt thrown over the back. I love color; lots, and *lots* of color. I love plants—lush, green plants must be in every room. My children collect rocks, crystals, pinecones, and feathers, so the windowsills and shelves are lined with this natural loot.

I love scents. I have a scented wax warmer in the living room, and every few days, I choose a new scent. I have three dogs, so this is a way I wash, freshen, and add aroma to the whole house.

Bathing the dogs and their bedding on a regular schedule helps. I put large, old beach towels down in the entryways during winter when there is a lot of mud tracked in.

We do not wear shoes in the house in order to help keep the floors clean for longer periods of time.

I like to keep my cleaning supplies stocked. The following is a list of what I generally keep on hand:

Several gallons of white vinegar

5 lb. bag baking soda

2 huge boxes Surf laundry soap

2 gallons Dawn dish soap

Ajax scouring powder

Jug of Fabuloso cleaning solution (lavender scent)

Mr. Clean (fresh scent)

Gallon of bleach

Many spray bottles

Chapter 4

Stocking the Pantry and Frugal, Tasty Recipes

I love groceries. I love to cook and feed people, especially my family. I am also into prepping these days.

When I would look up prepping, I would find crazy preppers yelling about the apocalypse and storing up freeze-dried foods and guns. Fortunately, I then found homemakers and homesteaders doing what our great-grandmothers did on the farms to ensure that the family made it through long winters. Stocking pantries. Normal behavior.

A stocked pantry is so important in many ways. First off, if someone loses a job and you have a year's worth of pantry food stored, that buys you a lot of time before you must worry about feeding the family. That is a considerable weight off your shoulders during hard times. Second, it is like a personal grocery store. I love having everything I need right there at hand. I could go without shopping or leaving the house for weeks and still make nutritious and tasty dishes.

I cook from scratch more than ever right now in order to save money. We went over our budget, and I am trying to work with a $300 grocery envelope.

I do know that $300 goes far at a store like WinCo. If you buy all bulk foods and produce in season -- mostly flour, potatoes, onions, canned vegetables, and beans, then you will be happily shocked at how much you will load into your car. With $300, I have fed my family well for a month and even did a little bit of pantry stocking.

I stick to buying beans, rice, flour, canned beans, and vegetables. In the produce section, I stick to cabbage, big bags of onions and potatoes (that is the less expensive way), big bags of carrots, bananas, then bags of oranges and apples if in season. In the summer we enjoy more variety as produce is fresh, in season and cheap.

If you are a meat-eater, go for the whole chicken. You can bake it and then chop it up or shred it to put into many dishes. A whole chicken could last us a week if sectioned properly. You can also get ground beef in bulk and package it up to freeze. You only need a little for sauces and dishes.

I think casseroles are the best way to stretch food. Rice, beans, and potatoes are another way to extend the meals and fill bellies with nutritious food. When you read our grandparents' memoirs, you'll find that they lived on fried potatoes and onions, beans with a little bacon, and dandelion greens fried with bacon as well. Bacon does make everything taste good. Being vegetarian, it is the one thing I miss. You can buy a package of inexpensive bacon, freeze it, and use a little in soups, beans, greens, and so on to flavor many dishes.

If you are struggling, please look into food stamps, and if you have small children, you will qualify for WIC.

In the book *We Had Everything But Money,* one man talks about the hard times during the Depression when he was a child, and his father could not find work for a year. The father used some insurance money to pay the mortgage so they would not lose the house, and with the savings, he stocked up on 25 lb. crates of pasta, 25 lb. bags of flour, and beans. The father planted hundreds of tomato plants in their yard and in the lot next to their house. The mother canned all summer. They ate pasta with tomato sauce four times a week and the rest of the time they ate pasta in garlic and oil or pasta and beans. The man still remembers these dishes fondly.

Today we are so spoiled with foods in every color, flavor, and style. We have so many premade foods that we can just microwave or shake in a pan to reheat. We get bored quickly. It seems we need to be entertained by our meals as much as by our media.

But during the Depression, our great-grandparents (or grandparents depending on our age) lived on a few simple foods such as the fried potatoes and onions, beans, home baked breads, and greens. Seasonings were simple too. You can flavor everything with onions, garlic, and a little bacon grease.

I have been making simpler meals, and I am always surprised when my family seems to enjoy these the most.

Here is a collection of all the dishes and drinks I have made over the years. Those of you that have several of my books will recognize many of these recipes. Some are vegan, and some are for meat-eaters. You can add meat to the vegan dishes or veganize the meat dishes—some of them, not all of them. I also will share how I stock my pantry. I enjoyed pantry stocking but devoted myself to the craft after the first sheltering-in during the pandemic of spring 2020. The shelves were empty for the first time, and I could not find a bag of rice or pintos for months. I don't mess around now.

Stocking the Pantry Well for a Family of Four

My pantry looks like this today. I have always kept bulk foods, but lately, I am very stocked up. I do some premixed foods if they are cheaper.

Last year, I spent around $2,000 over a couple of months to fully stock my pantry. I stocked the food pantry, cleaning supplies, toiletries, and pet food. I purchased from Sam's Club, WinCo Foods, and Grocery Outlet. Costco was too crazy around that time. Azure Standard was running out of everything. I worked from the places I could get things. Some things listed here were all I could get in place of flour or beans at the time but may not be ordinary stock up items.

I highly recommend two books: *A Year Without The Grocery Store: A Step by Step Guide to Acquiring, Organizing, and Cooking Food Storage* by Karen Morris and *Prepper's Pantry* by Daisy Luther. Especially the latter by Luther. Daisy Luther knows her stuff and goes into detail on the hows and whys of preparing a pantry.

She teaches how to stock a year's worth of food in three months. She covers all the bases such as taking into account whether you are on food stamps or have limited funds, as well as what to do if you cannot afford organics. She talks about pesticides, GMOs, and the importance of filtered water. I recommend spending the money on this book if you are serious about prepping.

My Pantry

It is important to create a pantry that your family will enjoy and eat from, so only stock up on foods that you will eat. Keep nutrition high at the top of the list.

In *Prepper's Pantry*, Luther lists the amount of food one person consumes over a year. The grain amount nearly gave me a heart attack.

Here are the amounts for one person over the age of seven:

Grains: 300 lbs.

Beans: 60 lbs.

Dry milk: 75 lbs.

Sugars: 60 lbs.

Fats: 15 lbs.

Fruits and vegetables: 1,500 servings (combo of dried, canned, and fresh)

So, let us look at this quickly, and you can decide. I do not think we will need 1,200 lbs. of grains for our family of four. I am hoping not because I have no way of storing that amount of grain, much less wrapping my brain around that amount. However, it *is* a combination of rice, flour, pasta, oats, and other grains. It is not just 1,200 lbs. of rice. Whew.

For a family of four, you would need 240 lbs. of beans. I can agree with this as we are mostly vegetarian. The beans would be a combination of pinto, black bean, kidney, black-eyed peas, cannellini, lentils...you name it.

Dry milk can be replaced with oats or organic soybeans. You can make soy milk, oat milk, or even nut milks. I use oat milk for cooking and baking, and it is excellent.

We love sugar, but I would never need even one serving of 60 lbs., and 240 lbs. would last decades. We use sugar for baking, and we use honey or monk fruit to sweeten our tea and coffee. I bake sweets once every two weeks, and lately I've been trying to do that even less as we are trying to reduce our consumption of sweets. Perhaps a 20 lb. bag of sugar for the year will suffice.

Let us look at the last item on the list: produce. I can agree with this amount. We love our produce and hunger for the fresh stuff. Canned and frozen produce is fine, but you would rely on canned if you do not have much freezer space. So, mastering year-round gardening is the other option. Then you are able to can your produce year-round as well.

Dried Foods

50 lb. all-purpose flour for tortillas, Amish bread, wheat bread, and crackers

25 lb. wheat flour for wheat bread and wheat tortillas (when feeling really healthy)

20 plus bags and boxes of pasta of all sorts (spaghetti, macaroni, shells, linguini)

20 lb. ancient grains flour (all I could find for a few months)

60 lb. white rice

25 lb. brown rice

50 lb. pinto beans

25 lb. black beans

25 lb. garbanzos

50 lb. oats (for milk, cream, or flour)

25 lb. steel cut oats

20 lb. red lentils

20 lb. kidney beans

20 lb. organic soybeans (soy milk, tofu)

20 lb. brown lentils (for vegan sloppy joes, lentil loaf, Indian soups)

20 lb. Krusteaz Pancake Mix (great for when you have no ingredients like eggs or milk)

20 small boxes of Jiffy cornbread mix (I would buy double since it takes four boxes to make a big pan)

20 boxes generic macaroni and cheese (you could double that)

Dried fruit

Nuts

Peanut butter or nut butters

Other Dried Goods For Baking and Vegan Foods

Large bags of tapioca (good for vegan cheese)

Gluten wheat (for making gluten faux meats)

Cornmeal

Corn starch

Baking powder

Vanilla extract

Brown sugar

White sugar

Maple syrup

Active Dry Yeast

Baking soda

Cinnamon

Powdered eggs

Powdered milk

Ghee

Canned Goods

I did not can at all this year. Here is what I purchased from the store:

Green beans

Corn

Creamed corn

Ranch style beans

Baked beans

Cream of mushroom

Mushroom gravy

Olives

Green enchilada sauce

Red enchilada sauce

Canned tomato sauce

Canned diced tomatoes

Applesauce

Coconut milk

Cranberry jelly

Seasonings and Sauces (regular and vegan pantry):

Sriracha
Salt
Ground black pepper
White pepper
Italian seasoning
Fennel powder
Cayenne powder
Tajin (great with lime juice on fruit)
Garlic powder
Onion powder
Oregano
Basil
Parsley
Bay leaves
Cumin
Smoked paprika
Turmeric
Masalas
Nutritional yeast
Vinegars: white, rice, and wine
Coconut oil
Sesame oil
Olive oil

Frozen Foods:

Mixed vegetables
Broccoli
Berries and fruit
Alternative meats if vegan

Whole chickens
Packages of ground beef

Refrigerator:

Ketchup (OrganicVille is a good one that we love)
Relish
Mustard
Coconut aminos
Greens
Veggies
Fruit
Milk (cow, goat, nut, or oat)
Butter (cow or vegan)
Mayonnaise (Vegenaise for vegan)
Hoisin Sauce
Chili garlic sauce
Sweet chili sauce
Pickles (whole dill and sliced bread and butter)
Olives (whatever you like, we love garlic stuffed)

Baskets:

Potatoes: Yukon gold, Idaho, red, yams
Tomatoes
Avocados
Ginger
Onions
Garlic

Lemons and limes

I also shop huge sales. I will buy healthy, dry cereals to have on hand and other canned or boxed items.

What Do I Cook?

I bake a lot of bread these days. I used to splurge on store-bought, but we like good bread, which runs about $3 on the low end and $4.99 on average. I can make a loaf for 50 cents to $1. The boys have hearty appetites, and breakfast is simple with thick slices of homemade bread slathered with homemade vegan butter and jam or honey. Sometimes we mash avocados on the toast if I find a sale. I used to make a few loaves a week, but now I feel like I bake six loaves a week.

I am working on learning the craft of soups. I love a minestrone recipe I got from *Simply Sara Kitchen* on YouTube, and I could make a delicious chicken soup, but I am struggling with vegetarian soups.

The easiest way to feed the family for the day and not spend all day in the kitchen is to use your crockpot, Instant Pot, or make a large pot of soup to put on the stove to simmer.

We have so many fancy mixed and prepared food nowadays. But dinner does not have to be so complicated. We do one big meal in the middle of the day made up of a salad, a sautéed vegetable, a starch like rice or pasta, then a protein such as beans or tofu or alternative meat.

I've finally mastered chili. It took years, but I can make the best chili; so I make a huge pot, and we eat it with tortillas, then when we get bored, we make it into burritos. Sometimes I make chili and cheese burritos. I veganize everything. I know this is not for everyone.

I do use alternative cheeses and meat, but do so very sparingly.

I can make alternative cheeses, meats, bologna for sandwiches, milks, and butter right in my kitchen in just a few hours. I can make a gallon of oat milk for $1. A gallon of homemade soy milk is maybe $2. In the store, a half-gallon is $4.99.

I can make cheese and cheese sauce with cashews, nutritional yeast, and other ingredients. I can make butter with coconut oil, lecithin, and soy milk. With tofu and gluten, I can make bologna for sandwiches. I can make gluten with wheat and wheat gluten and make faux chicken and faux steak that is delicious.

We love these dishes and make most of them for less than $1. I can make a pan of gluten steaks for a few dollars, whereas a pan of real steak would be $20 or more, depending on the cut.

We also make homemade pizza. Sometimes the frozen or boxed variety of certain foods can be cheaper to purchase, such as pizza and macaroni and cheese. But with homemade, I have the ingredients on hand, and we avoid a lot of strange chemicals.

As I learn how to make more foods from scratch, I enjoy the kitchen work and can cook in bulk, so the rest of the week is easy. You can make mixes and extra dishes for the pantry and freezer. I would shop on Saturday morning and spend Sunday cooking and baking most of the day. Cooking from scratch helps you prepare foods free from dyes, chemicals, preservatives, extra sugar, fat, and salt. You will also save so much money. Homemade food is much more nutritious than store-bought or fast food.

My family is not vegan, but they eat what I cook. I am not the perfect vegan or even vegetarian. I do my best. I love eating this way and feel so much better physically. I also enjoy the creativity of veganizing all of our favorite dishes, but that gets pricey with the alternative meats, cheeses, and milk. So, I have learned to make my own, and it is cheap!

Here are my tried and true tasty recipes for some significant savings. Some recipes are mine that I have altered from other recipes, and others were found online and from other books. I will refer to or link the sources.

Soy Milk

Source: The New Farm Vegetarian Cookbook by Louise Hagler

You can buy 25 lb. bags of organic soybeans at a local health food store or co-op.

Soak 2 ½ cups soybeans in 5 cups cold water for 8 to 10 hours (in the refrigerator if weather is hot). Rinse and then add 1 cup of the soybeans with 2 ½ cups of water in blender and blend well. Add mixture to a large pot or double boiler until all the beans and water are blended.

Simmer over medium heat. When liquid begins to boil, turn down and simmer over low heat for 20 minutes. Keep an eye on it and occasionally stir as the foam will rise suddenly and overflow. After 20 minutes, strain the liquid in a cheesecloth. You can blend again with dates, some vanilla, honey, or whatever you like. The soy milk lasts 3 to 5 days. You can make a gallon for a dollar. In the store, it cost $3.99 to $4.99 for a half-gallon!

Oat Milk

There are so many recipes for oat milk on YouTube. I combined a few recipes.

You need 1 cup of oats and 3 cups of water. You can add dates (I like to soak the dates for a few hours, but make sure you don't soak the oats). You can add a small amount of cashews to thicken. Blend well and strain with a cheesecloth over a pot. Add a little salt, vanilla, and some sweetener, or leave it plain. It does not last more than a few days, so make this a small amount at a time. You can make a half gallon for under a dollar if you do not use dates. In the store, you are paying $3 to $4 for the same amount of oat milk.

Bologna

Source: www.itdoesnttastelikechicken.comhttps://itdoesnttastelikechicken.com/vegan-baloney-bologna/

Ingredients

1 block (350g) extra-firm tofu, drained

½ cup ketchup

¼ cup nutritional yeast

3 tablespoons soy sauce

1 ½ tablespoons onion powder

1 ½ tablespoons garlic powder

1 tablespoon smoked paprika

1 tablespoon mustard powder

¼ teaspoon nutmeg

1 ¾ cups vital wheat gluten

Instructions

Add several inches of water to a large pot with a steamer basket and bring to a boil.

1. In a food processor, add the tofu, ketchup, nutritional yeast, soy sauce, onion powder, garlic powder, smoked paprika, mustard powder, and nutmeg. Mix until smooth as possible, stopping to scrape the sides as needed. Add the vital wheat gluten and pulse several times to incorporate, scraping the sides as needed. It will form a crumbly dough.

2. Turn the mixture out onto a clean work surface and knead together to form a dough. Shape into a large log that will fit in your steamer basket. Roll the log up in foil, twisting the ends closed, so it looks like a large candy. Place in the steamer basket and cover. Steam for 1 hour. The vegan bologna will have expanded in the foil, making a tight log.

3. Remove from the steamer basket and allow it to cool. Move to refrigerator and chill thoroughly before serving. When ready to serve, just slice and enjoy! Store in the refrigerator in an airtight container for up to 1 week.

Gluten

Gluten is a chewy food used to make faux sweet and sour pork, faux chicken, and mock steak.

Source: The New Farm Vegetarian Cookbook by Louise Hagler

You will need 8 cups of flour: half white or wheat flour and half gluten flour. You can do it with just the wheat and white and no gluten flour, but it is less chewy in texture.

Mix with 3 to 4 cups of water and knead for 10 to 15 minutes until it forms a big dough ball that stretches and bounces back when poked. Let soak in a pan of water for an hour.

You will have to knead the dough in water and rinse several times. The water will be very milky. The recipe instructions say to knead it until the water is clear, but I have never had that experience. The dough ball will be smaller in the end after you have washed most of the starch out.

Cut in a few pieces and boil in a broth. I do the suggested vegetable broth with chopped onion, soy sauce, and oil. Simmer for an hour. The book suggests thickening the broth for gravy, but I have not tried doing that yet.

You can store the gluten and slice as needed.

Gluten Steak

I love this mock steak and, after fiddling around with a few recipes, I came up with this one. You can alter it to your liking.

Heat oil and sauté about ½ cup of finely chopped onions in a pan.

Slice gluten and add to pan, pouring Worcestershire sauce and BBQ sauce over it. Simmer for several minutes. Turn to cook on both sides. Add more seasoning if needed.

Sauté more onions and mushrooms in another pan with some soy sauce, oil, and a little more Worcestershire sauce if you're up for it.

Add mushrooms and some onion mix on top of steaks and enjoy. I love this dish.

Stretchy, Gooey Cheese

Source:
www.itdoesnttastelikechicken.comhttps://itdoesnttastelikechicken.com/melty-stretchy-gooey-vegan-mozarella/

Ingredients

½ cup raw cashews, softened (see step 1)

1 cup water

3 tablespoons + 2 teaspoons tapioca starch (also called tapioca flour)

1 tablespoon nutritional yeast

1 teaspoon apple cider vinegar

½ teaspoon salt

¼ teaspoon garlic powder

Instructions

Soften the cashews by soaking for 4 hours or overnight. This is especially important for a creamy cheese.

To make the vegan mozzarella:

1. Add the cashews along with the 1 cup of water and all the remaining ingredients to a blender. Blend until completely smooth. It will be very watery.

2. Pour into a small saucepan and cook over medium-high heat. Continually stir. The cheese will start forming

clumps, keep stirring, and it will continue clumping until the mixture turns from watery to a thicker melty cheese sauce. This takes about 5 minutes. Serve hot or allow to cool and store in an air-tight container in the fridge for 2-3 days. The cheese will get thicker as it cools but will stay in a melty state.

We love this cheese. It is amazing!

Vegan Butter

Recipe found in The Homemade Vegan Pantry by Miyoko Schinner. I make this weekly, and we love this butter more than any store-bought. It would help if you kept it refrigerated or it goes bad quickly since there are no preservatives in it.

1 ½ cup refined coconut oil (I melt it)

½ cup soy milk or soy cream

¼ cup oil (canola, grapeseed, peanut, or olive)

½ teaspoon salt (we love salt and use a full teaspoon)

2 teaspoons lecithin (I use liquid)

Place all ingredients in a blender and blend for about one minute to make sure that everything is properly incorporated. Pour into a bowl or container with lid and let it set in the refrigerator until solid.

Vegan Chili

I am not a chili person, but we love this recipe. It does require some alternative store-bought plant meats, but you do not need much, and when we find them on sale or discount at a Grocery Outlet, we stock up and use them sparingly.

In a pan with oil, sauté one package of Beyond Beef Crumbles. Add one package of Beyond Hot Italian Sausage cut up into bite sized pieces. Sauté on low for approximately 5 minutes.

Cook up a pot of pinto beans. Pintos quadruple in size, so pay attention to the water. I pour four or more cups of dry beans in a pot and enough water to be two inches over the beans. You can soak overnight if you'd like. It is supposed to help with gas, but I have not found this to be true. Beans need to simmer for at least a couple of hours. When they are soft, you then add salt and seasoning.

Beans will expand like crazy as they cook, so keep adding water if you need to, but not too much. You do not want water chili. You want thick chili. So maybe keep it at an inch above the beans.

To the beans, add salt, oregano, chili seasoning (whatever is your favorite), garlic powder, and smoked paprika to your liking. I cannot tell you how much. I add a LOT. Start with a tablespoon of each and keep adding. Remember, you can always add more, but you cannot take it out.

You can also add the same seasoning to the faux meat as you cook it.

Add faux meat to beans and simmer for an hour. Add any toppings you would like (optional) or enjoy as is.

Super Fast, Cheap, and Easy Dinners:

My favorite meal starts off with a few boxes of a generic macaroni and cheese I find at Grocery Outlet. I veganize it somewhat (still use the cheese powder) with a plain unsweetened soy milk and vegan butter.

Next, I sauté a large panful of frozen mixed vegetables (corn, carrots, peas, and green beans). I sauté a chopped onion in a little oil first until it is a bit golden, then add the vegetables. When it is all cooked, I add a little bit of vegan butter, salt, and black pepper.

Half the plate is filled with veggies, a quarter of it with an easy green salad, and a quarter of it with macaroni and cheese. So good, and so filling.

Another thing I like to do is to chop golden potatoes in quarters and boil. I then drain and serve with gravy poured over them. I use Campbell's mushroom gravy. Serve with a side of steamed broccoli or green salad.

We eat a lot of beans—pinto, black, kidney, garbanzo, and lentils. But Bali cooks them Indian style, so they are loaded with flavor.

Indian Style Beans and Lentils:

In a big pot, add beans or lentils, water (an inch or two over, keep an eye on it), chopped onion, tomato, garlic, fresh ginger, a teaspoon or tablespoon of turmeric, curry powder, and salt. Boil until done. In a pan, add oil and sauté a bit more onion until golden and add to the pot. You can also add masala purchased from an Indian grocery store. Chana Masala is for garbanzos (chickpeas); rajmah masala is for kidney beans. You can buy meat masalas as well. For all other beans, just use curry powder.

That is all you do for flavorful beans.

We serve them with white rice, brown rice, or tortillas.

Mashed Potatoes:

You will need:

Potatoes (any potato will do, but Yukon gold is the richest and yummiest)
Plain and unsweetened soy milk
Vegan butter (optional and tastes great without)
Nutritional yeast
Onion powder
Garlic powder
Salt and pepper to taste

Boil potatoes, drain, and place back into the pot. Use a cake beater to whip them until creamy. You can add even more seasonings if you feel daring.

Corn and Brussels Sprouts:

My kids love this! I love this! You can substitute vegetable broth for the oil and butter.

Ingredients

Frozen corn

Fresh brussels sprouts

Earth Balance vegan butter

Coconut oil

Garlic

Salt

White pepper

Method

In a large pan, sauté garlic in coconut oil and butter. Don't toast or burn, just heat to release the essence of the garlic. Add frozen corn.

Wash and cut brussels sprouts in half and add to pan. Don't cook them too long.

Add more butter, salt and pepper. Serve.

Vegan Tostadas From Heaven

This dish is so easy and fast.

Ingredients

Homemade or canned refried beans (I sometimes add my

favorite canned beans: Ranch Style Beans and S&W Chili Beans)

Tostadas

Lettuce

Tomatoes

Homemade vegan thousand island dressing

Sriracha

Method

I usually make refried beans and throw in a can of the S&W Chili and Ranch Style beans to make it fabulous. Mash it all up.

Top tostadas with beans, shredded lettuce, chopped tomatoes and then drizzle generously with thousand island dressing and Sriracha.

Homemade Vegan Thousand Island

I combined three different recipes here. There is Worcestershire sauce in mine and that is not vegan (I was disappointed). But there is a vegan substitute, yay!

Ingredients

1 cup Vegenaise

1 Tbsp Annie's Worcestershire sauce (vegan, baby!)

2 Tbsp ketchup

1 Tbsp lemon juice (fresh)

2 Tbsp relish

1 Tbsp minced garlic (jarred is best for strong flavor)

1 Tbsp red onion, minced

Salt to taste

White pepper to taste

Vinegar is optional (I don't use it)

Directions

In a large bowl, mix all ingredients until combined.

Store in a jar and keep refrigerated.

It gets better each day, as the flavors marinate. I sort of eyeball the measurements and add to taste, so this is truly a foundation recipe. Experiment to make it to your liking. Add more lemon or pepper, if you wish. You can even spice it up with a little Sriracha.

Sometimes I just drizzle this dressing on lettuce leaves and eat them like an appetizer. I eat a head of lettuce almost daily.

Best Homemade Beans:

I usually just cook black or pinto beans. This is another way I like to make them. Super easy.

First, clean, sort, and wash a few cups' worth of dry beans and place in a pot with a couple of inches of water covering them.

Bring them to a boil and then turn off the heat and let them sit overnight.

The next day, mince a whole bulb of garlic and toss it in with salt to taste and let them simmer for a couple of hours on low, or until fully cooked.

If you want refried beans, you can use black or pinto, but pinto is the common refried bean. Just cook in a crockpot all day and only keep a little bit of water covering the beans. The less water you add, the thicker the refried beans will be. When they are super tender, mash them up. This may take a few rounds of mashing, stirring, and letting simmer more.

Homemade Tortillas (source: www.tasteofhome.com)

These are so darn good that I gained an extra five pounds enjoying them. I ate them with big pots of beans, and anything else I could conjure up that would go with these delicious tortillas.

They are so quick and easy and cost something crazy like 50 cents per batch compared to $3 or more per bag at the store, and they are fresh, hot, and chewy. You will not go back. I usually double or triple the batch and store in the fridge. They will last a few days.

Ingredients

2 cups white flour (you can use half wheat, if you'd like)

½ teaspoon salt

¾ cup water

3 Tbsp oil

Directions

In a large bowl, add all ingredients.

Mix and knead, adding more flour or water if necessary. Let sit for 20 minutes.

Make into small balls and roll out onto a floured surface.

In a large skillet, cook tortillas over medium heat for approximately 1 minute on each side, or until lightly brown.

Keep and serve warm.

Martha Stewart's One Pot Pasta

I used to make this when we used chicken broth and it was incredibly delicious. I now just use vegetable broth instead. The recipe calls for water, but I find that a broth makes it 10 times yummier.

Ingredients

12 oz linguine pasta

1 onion, chopped

½ tsp pepper flakes

2 Tbsp olive oil

4 ½ cups vegetable broth (you can also make a faux chicken broth)

12 oz cherry or grape tomatoes, chopped in half or quartered

4 cloves fresh garlic, minced

2 sprigs basil

Salt and pepper to taste

Directions

Place all ingredients in a pot and bring to a boil.

Reduce heat and stir occasionally until all the water or broth is absorbed by the pasta.

Stovetop Vegan Pizza

This dish is a combination of recipes. Both *High Carb Hannah* and Nikki over at www.chef-in-training.com have versions, but you may top it however you like. This dish works well with my gas stove; it seems easier to make, and I love the thick, pan style.

There are a few parts to this pizza.

The Perfect Pizza Dough (source: www.chef-in-training.com)

Ingredients

2 cups warm water

1 Tbsp active dry yeast

1 Tbsp salt

5 cups flour

Directions

Add yeast to warm water and let sit for 5 minutes.

Add half the flour and mix well, pour onto floured board

and mix in remainder.

Knead and return to bowl to sit covered with a towel for 20 minutes.

She gets a bit fancier, but I find simple works as well.

Pizza Assembly

Method

Sprinkle cornmeal on bottom of a large skillet.

Press dough into the pan to completely cover the bottom.

Add sauce and toppings of your choice.

We love tons of olives, corn, red onions, and pineapple. Go easy on sliced tomatoes if you decide to use them, as they make the dough soggy. Be careful not to use too much sauce for this same reason.

If you would like a vegan cheese, *High Carb Hannah* on YouTube has a good recipe for one:

Ingredients

¼ cup cashews

3 Tbsp nutritional yeast

½ Tbsp granulated or powdered garlic, or to taste

Himalayan pink salt, to taste

Directions

Blend all ingredients in a blender.

Sprinkle on pizza.

Place pan on stove and cover with a tight-fitting lid.

Cook on low for approximately 15 minutes. This part is tricky; sometimes it's taken up to 30 minutes if there are lots of watery toppings. Keep an eye on it.

When it is fully cooked, place it on a chopping board, cut and serve. So good.

Makes 2 pan pizzas.

Asian Noodle Soup

There is some controversy as to whether this is really considered vegan. I use a pho soup mix or wonton soup mix. The beef and chicken are artificial flavors and I've seen Rose from *Cheap Lazy Vegan* on YouTube eat artificially flavored chicken ramen. This is for you to decide. You can also just use an alternative vegan broth.

I just boil a huge pot of water with the soup seasoning, rice noodles, and tons of greens. Sometimes I get all this from our local Korean store, so I have no idea what the greens are called. We eat the soup in huge bowls that I also purchased there, and we use chopsticks because it's fun.

This is a great soup for cold days. You leave the table feeling warm, full, and fortified.

Packed Veggie Eggless Rolls

I make these now and then, and they are a hit, even with my elderly neighbors who love their meat. They are very high in fat, so this is a treat.

Ingredients

Egg roll wraps (get the soft, large ones)

Vegetables (red and green cabbage, carrots, onions, bean sprouts)

Veri Veri Teriyaki Sauce

Oil (a light oil for frying)

Dipping sauce of choice (I use sweet chili sauce)

Water for steaming

Directions

Shred vegetables in a food processor or grate and chop by hand. You can add whatever else you would like, such as tofu or other vegetables.

In a wok or large pan, add vegetables and a bit of water.

Put the lid on to steam for a short period. You want the vegetables to be cooked, but still be a bit crunchy.

Drain, return to pan, and add Veri Veri Teriyaki sauce.

Lay the wrap on a dry surface and put a large amount of vegetables in the middle, then wrap it like a burrito and seal with a dab of water. I like to make batches, so they are fresh and crunchy.

In a large, deep pan, add about an inch of oil. Let the oil get hot, but not boiling, *crazy* hot.

Use tongs to carefully add egg rolls and turn as needed until golden brown.

Place on a platter with paper towels to absorb all the oil.

Serve with dipping sauce.

You can also choose different sauces, we just like Thai sweet chili sauce.

Faux Tuna Salad (source: www.revolutioninbloom.com)

1-15 oz can cooked garbanzo beans

½ cup diced dill pickles

½ cup diced celery

½ diced red onion

1 or 2 Tbsp nori sheets ground to flakes

Vegenaise (as much as you like)

Salt to taste

Pepper to taste

Add garbanzo beans to a food processor and pulse a few times, keeping them a bit textured, and not pasty. You want a sort of flaky texture. Pour into bowl.

Mix in all remaining ingredients and you're done.

I have taken to adding other things such as mustard and fresh lemon juice. Others like cayenne or other seasonings.

This recipe is very flexible. You can adjust all the ingredients to your liking; adding more of this, and less of that. I found we liked a ton of nori flakes and extra salt. This is a very good dish to eat on crackers and in sandwiches.

I usually double the batch.

Green Smoothie

Ingredients

Frozen bananas

Frozen berries (optional)

Almond or soy milk

Greens (best for smoothies are kale, spinach, dandelion greens, collards, and chard)

A Vitamix works best for these smoothies, but any good one will do.

Method

Start by blending the greens and milk.

Next, add bananas and frozen berries or any other fruit, one by one. Do this until it has reached the sweetness and creaminess you love.

Mangos and pineapple are good, too. You don't need to use all these greens in one smoothie.

Mix and match or just use one at a time.

Green Juice (Sometimes Red):

This recipe is very simple.

Ingredients

Apples

Fresh lemon, peeled

Fresh ginger, peeled

Cucumber

Carrots

Celery

Greens

Beets

Method

Juice all ingredients according to juicer manufacturer's directions.

You decide the amount of fruits and vegetables you want to juice. We like to use extra carrots and apples to make it a bit sweeter for the kids. If you are trying to detox from metals such as aluminum in vaccines, throw in cilantro and parsley each time.

Get the cheapest apples. When you juice them, it doesn't matter if they are old. See if your health food store marks down older produce. Perhaps they are willing to give it to you for compost. If so, take it home and then salvage what you can. My old co-op used to have boxes of reduced produce daily. I liked to buy bags of it and use it for juicing because even if it's bruised or funky, it all becomes juice.

Desserts and Coffee

What is life without sweets and coffee? Not much to me. Here are some vegan desserts, and one is even healthy! I'll also share my best coffee secrets.

Vegan Vanilla Cake (source: www.lovingitvegan.com)

Ingredients

1 ¾ cups all-purpose flour

1 cup sugar

1 tsp baking soda

½ tsp salt

1 cup plain soy milk

2 tsp vanilla extract

1/3 cup olive oil (I use coconut oil)

1 Tbsp white vinegar

Directions

In a large bowl, mix wet ingredients.

In another, mix dry ingredients.

Combine the two, and pour in a baking pan.

Bake in a preheated oven at 350 degrees Fahrenheit for 30 minutes or until a toothpick inserted in the middle comes out clean.

Vegan Vanilla Buttercream Frosting (source: www.elizabethrider.com)

Ingredients

1 cup Earth Balance butter

3 cups powdered sugar

2 tsp soy or almond milk

¾ tsp vanilla extract

Note: For chocolate buttercream I replace 1 cup of powdered sugar with 1 cup of cacao powder.

Directions

Whip until creamy.

Store in refrigerator in an airtight container for up to 7 days.

Chocolate Cake:

This is from a regular homemade cake recipe that a neighbor gave me. I just converted it to a healthier vegan version (if cake can be considered healthy). I always use coconut oil in my cakes because it makes the cake heavier, moister, and gooey.

Preheat oven to 350 degrees Fahrenheit.

Ingredients

2 cups coconut sugar

2 ½ cups flour

1 cup cacao (better for you than cocoa, you choose)

2 tsp salt

1 cup coconut oil

1 cup water

1 cup unsweetened plain soy milk

2 TBSP vinegar

2 tsp vanilla

Method

I like to mix my wet and dry ingredients separately and then combine them with a hand mixer. Pour into a nonstick or greased cake pan and bake for about 35 minutes or until a toothpick inserted in the middle comes out clean.

CHEF AJ's Black Bean Chocolate Brownies (source: *CHEF AJ* on YouTube)

These brownies are super healthy! I let my boys eat these some mornings for fun.

Ingredients

2 cups rinsed black beans, cooked

¾ cup oats (you can grind into flour or leave whole)

1 cup date syrup (I use Date Lady)

½ cup cocoa (I use cacao; it's healthier)

1 tsp baking powder

½ tsp baking soda

Chocolate chips, as little or as much as you want (enjoy life!)

Directions

Place all ingredients in a food processor, pulse a few times, until combined. Pour into a baking pan. I like to use my cast iron skillet and then cover the top with dark chocolate chips. Sometimes I'll add sprinkles for fun. Bake in a preheated oven at 350 degrees Fahrenheit for 20-30 minutes, depending on the size of your pan.

Kate's Fancy Espresso Coffee

I don't drink this every day, or I'd have even more weight to lose.

Ingredients

Espresso

Milk

Water

Method

Make a strong cup of espresso in a stovetop Italian espresso maker. Pour into a large mug, add some hot water and a large scoop of Nature's Charm Sweetened Condensed Coconut Milk. This is a treat!

Use as much or as little espresso, water, and milk as you want.

Great Chefs To Keep You Inspired

Here is a list of some creative vegan chefs on YouTube to help you make amazing dishes and keep everyone happy. Even the meat eaters may find their happy place on the plate.

MommyTang
High Carb Hannah
It Doesn't Taste Like Chicken
CHEF AJ
Edgy Veg
The Veggie Nut
avantgardevegan
The Happy Pear (great for kid-friendly vegan foods)
The Vegan Zombie
Cheap Lazy Vegan (fantastic for quick, cheap, and even some junk food)
Savvy Vegan (great for gluten-free recipes including fantastic 2 ingredient bread as well as pancakes)

Vitamin Deficiencies

You may want to take extra vitamin B12 and vitamin D. These are hard to get without the processed dairy and meat.

Eating a wide variety of vegetables, fruits, grains, legumes, nuts, and seeds will cover everything else. Educate yourself so you are giving your family the best chance at having vibrant health.

Easy Dishes

Slow Cooker Potatoes

Wash a bag of potatoes and fill up your large slow cooker, as many as will comfortably fit inside.

Cook on high heat for 4 to 6 hours.

Just poke a potato with a fork to see if it is soft.
I store them in the refrigerator once they cool. You can reheat them for days as baked and loaded potatoes or turn them into fried potatoes and onions.

Potatoes & Onions

Preheat pan and add a couple of tablespoons of oil.

Slice an onion and sauté for a couple of minutes.

Add chopped, pre-cooked potatoes and let them get brown and a bit crispy.

Serve with pinto beans.

You can add whatever toppings or condiments you'd like. Sour cream and hot sauce are wonderful. I like to use ketchup on my fried potatoes.

Cornbread

I take a huge box of Krusteaz cornbread and make a big cake pan of it.

This can be served for a couple of days with a side salad, green beans or other vegetables. It goes perfectly with a bowl of home-cooked beans or chili, as well.

Here is a collection of family favorite recipes that I've been making over the years:

Peasant Bread

Ingredients

3 cups warm water

2 Tbsp yeast

5 cups white flour (you can substitute a cup for bran or flax)

2 or more cups wheat flour

Directions

In a large bowl, add 3 cups warm water (not *too* warm or it will kill the yeast) and sprinkle yeast in.

Add 5 cups white flour or 3 to 4 cups and 1 to 2 cups flax, bran, or whatever sounds good to you.

Stir, cover with a damp cloth, and let sit and rise for 1 hour.

Once risen, add the additional 2 cups of wheat flour and stir.

Pour onto a floured surface and knead it until it is no longer sticky. You may have to add more flour as you go.

Put back in the bowl and cover with the damp cloth. Let rise for another hour.

After the second rise, punch down and divide in half. Place each half into bread pans. Cover again for a third rise.

Bake in the oven at 350 degrees Fahrenheit for 35 to 50 minutes.

This recipe is very adaptable. You can add anything to change it. Some examples: nuts, dried raisins and cinnamon, butter and honey (that is what the original recipe calls for), or make it super healthy with all sorts of oat bran and wheat bran.

Amish White Bread (source: www.allrecipes.com)

Ingredients

2 cups warm water

2/3 cups sugar

1 ½ Tbsp active dry yeast

1 ½ tsp salt

¼ cup oil

6 cups white flour

Directions

In a large bowl, mix water and yeast and let sit for about 5 minutes.

Add sugar, oil, salt, and flour last.

Mix and pour out onto floured surface and knead until no longer sticky (may need to add more flour).

Return to bowl and cover with damp cloth and let rise for 1 hour.

Once risen, punch down and divide in half.

Make into loaves and put into pans.

Cover with damp cloth again and let rise once more.

Bake at 350 degrees Fahrenheit for 30 to 40 minutes.

Mushroom Stroganoff (source: *Simply Sara Kitchen* on YouTube)

Ingredients

1 lb button mushrooms, sliced (or any kind you prefer or whatever's on sale)

1 onion, diced

2 Tbsp olive oil

2 Tbsp butter

4 cloves minced garlic

1 Tbsp Worcestershire sauce

4 Tbsp white flour

3 cups vegetable stock

½ cup sour cream

¼ tsp thyme

Salt to taste

Granulated or powdered garlic to taste

Granulated or powdered onion to taste

Black pepper to taste

Directions

Sauté mushrooms and diced onions in the butter and oil until all the liquid from the mushrooms has cooked down/evaporated.

Add garlic and Worcestershire sauce and saute for about a minute.

Sprinkle in the white flour, cook, and stir a couple more minutes.

Add vegetable stock, stir.

Add all seasonings: salt, garlic powder, onion powder, pepper, and thyme.

Simmer on low heat and add sour cream.

This is so delicious over egg noodles. I eat too many helpings. Sometimes I double the batch, we love it so much. Hands down, this recipe is one of my favorites!

Spaghetti with French Bread

Ingredients

1 loaf French bread (or you can bake your own)

1 lb spaghetti pasta

2 (29 oz) cans Hunt's tomato sauce

1 lb package grass-fed ground beef

Italian seasoning to taste

A few tablespoons of olive oil (or whichever kind you prefer or have in your pantry)

Granulated or powdered garlic to taste

Granulated or powdered onion to taste

Salt to taste

Directions

sauté ground beef in pan with a little oil.

Add about 1 teaspoon each of garlic powder, onion powder, and Italian seasoning to the beef and cook until no longer pink or raw. You can drain the oil if you'd like, I usually do not.

Add Hunt's tomato sauce and add more garlic, onion, Italian seasoning, and salt to taste.

Simmer on very low for an hour.

Toward the end, cook pasta according to package directions, adding some olive oil and salt to the boiling water to prevent stickiness.

Serve sauce over pasta and add a nice hunk of French bread on the side.

Tuna Casserole

Ingredients

1 bag egg noodles

1 can tuna

1 can cream of mushroom

1 can cream of chicken

1Tbsp chicken bouillon

1 ½ cups milk (add more if it seems too thick)

2 cups grated cheddar cheese, or use what you prefer or have on hand

Directions

In a large pan, simmer milk, tuna, cream of mushroom, cream of chicken, and chicken bouillon (this is your sauce).

Next, boil pasta until al dente.

Put pasta in a casserole dish and pour sauce over it.

Sprinkle cheese on top.

Bake for about 35 minutes at 350 degrees Fahrenheit.

You can double or triple this recipe to feed a larger family. I double this for the four of us and to have lunch to pack for my husband.

Vegan Pizza

Ingredients

Pizza dough (recipe follows)

Spaghetti sauce or tomato sauce

Daiya mozzarella cheese (vegan alternative)

Canned black olives without pits

Tomatoes

Bell pepper

Red onions

Any other vegetables you like

Dough (source: www.chef-in-training.com, but I've simplified it)

Ingredients

2 cups warm water

1 Tbsp yeast

1 Tbsp salt (optional)

5 cups flour

Directions

Mix yeast with water and let it sit for 10 minutes.

Add flour and mix, pour out onto floured surface and knead, adding more flour if necessary.

Make into a ball and return to bowl, cover with a kitchen towel and let rest for up to 20 minutes.

Divide into two parts, roll into a ball and roll out for your pizza.

Slice vegetables thinly and chop up olives.

Spread sauce with the back of a spoon and sprinkle a thin layer of vegan cheese.

Layer on vegetables.

Bake for 14 minutes at 400 degrees Fahrenheit, or until pizza is light brown and bubbly.

Briar Rabbit Burritos (This is a Briar Patch Co-op vegan vegetable wrap)

With this one you can add or omit any vegetables you like and use vegan mayo, cream cheese (vegan or dairy), or hummus.

Ingredients

Large tortillas (wheat, white flour, or flavored such as tomato basil, spinach, etc.)

Mayo, hummus, and/or cream cheese (vegan or not)

Sprouts

Bell peppers

Tomatoes

Shredded carrots

Peppers

Spinach or lettuce

Cucumbers

Pickles

Directions

Lay out the tortilla and spread on the hummus, mayo, or cream cheese.

Add vegetables (any vegetable you like or is in season) in layers and add salt and pepper to taste.

Roll up like a burrito, cut in half, and devour.

Cooking Rice

If you have a rice cooker it is simply two parts water to one part rice (white or brown). If you have no rice cooker, then add rice and water to a pot and cover, simmer on low for around 20 minutes for white rice and 40 minutes for brown.

I like to add chicken bouillon to flavor my rice. You can add butter, herbs, and other seasonings. Knorr soup packages make it a bit Rice-A-Roni-ish.

Large Pans of Delicious Veggies

Ingredients

Garlic

Red or yellow onions

Bags of frozen vegetables of your choice

Olive oil (or whichever kind you prefer or have in your pantry)

Salt and pepper

Method

These vegetables can be cooked in a regular pan, or you can use a cast iron pan, if you have one. If you use the latter, heat the pan slowly and then add plenty of oil and heat that slowly as well.

Slice a few cloves of garlic and slice up a whole onion and add both to the pan and sauté until onions are beginning to brown a bit.

Add frozen vegetables and sauté for as long as it takes to heat through.

I stir now and then and don't fret it they look a bit grilled.

I love using the mixed vegetables with peas, corn, green beans and carrots, and a bag of various green beans, wax beans and carrots.

Serve over rice.

You can add a little Veri Veri Teriyaki, or any sauce, gravy, or eat as is. I also love this with macaroni and cheese. I just serve it side by side. So delicious and filling.

Baked Potato Fries

This method is a bit healthier than frying in oil.

Ingredients

Potatoes of your choice (we prefer Idaho russets)

Oil

Seasoning of your choice (garlic, salt, french fry seasoning, etc.)

Method

Wash and slice up your potatoes into steak fries sizes.

Toss with some oil and spread out on cookie sheets.

Sprinkle seasonings.

Bake at 400 degrees Fahrenheit for approximately 30 minutes.

They won't cook evenly, so just keep checking and when they are golden on the edges, taste one.

Slow Cooker Pot Roast

Ingredients

1 package of roasting meat, approximately 3-4 pounds

1 can cream of mushroom

1 packet of onion soup mix

5-6 potatoes chopped into small chunks

5-6 carrots chopped into small chunks

Any other vegetables you like (I love to use frozen corn and peas)

Directions

In a slow cooker, add everything plus enough water to cover.

Cook on low for 6-8 hours, or on high for 4-6 hours.

I usually double this recipe and have plenty for a couple days' worth of lunches and dinners.

Vegan Garden Pie (knockoff of Shepherd's pie, but my way)

Ingredients

1 can mushroom gravy, or any gravy (sometimes I use cream of mushroom as well)

1 package of Lightlife Smart Ground Crumbles or TVP sautéed in vegetable broth

1 lb bag of frozen peas and corn

½ onion, diced

Potatoes or potato flakes

Soy milk

Vegan butter

Oil

1 tsp garlic powder

1 tsp onion powder

Salt and pepper to taste

Directions

In a large skillet, sauté onions in a bit of oil for about 5 minutes, or until translucent.

Add crumbles or the reconstituted TVP.

Add gravy and a bag of frozen vegetables and cook until heated through.

Next, add the garlic and onion powder, salt and pepper.

In a separate pot, boil potatoes, then drain, mash, add butter, salt and soy milk.

You can also just boil water to make your powdered potatoes and cook according to package directions.

Spread potatoes on top of meat substitute and vegetable mixture and put in the oven to bake for 35 minutes at 350 degrees Fahrenheit.

I always double this recipe.

Minestrone Soup (source: *Simply Sara Kitchen* on YouTube)

Ingredients

2 Tbsp oil

2 Tbsp butter

1 onion, chopped

2 stalks celery, chopped

2 to 3 zucchini, chopped

4 tomatoes, chopped

4 to 5 cloves garlic, minced

1 (15 oz) can cannellini beans

1 (15 oz) can kidney beans

1 (15 oz) can black beans

4 cups water

1 cup frozen green beans

Handful of shredded carrots

1 Tbsp tomato paste

3 cups tomato juice

2 Tbsp vegetable bouillon

2 tsp parsley

1 tsp oregano

1 tsp basil

½ tsp thyme

Salt and pepper to taste

1 bag fresh spinach

Chunk of parmesan cheese

1 ¼ cup pasta shells

Directions

In a large skillet, sauté butter, oil, onion, celery, zucchini, and tomatoes.

Add garlic and cook for 1 minute.

Drain canned beans and add to skillet.

Add water, green beans, carrots, tomato paste, tomato juice, bouillon, herbs, salt, and pepper.

Stir well.

Add a few pieces of parmesan cheese and let it simmer for a while.

Add 1 ¼ cup pasta shells and cook until tender, about 7 minutes.

Next, add a bagful of fresh spinach.

This soup is SO delicious! It really does taste like Olive Garden's version, or better.

Potato and/or Salad Bar

This is for those days when you want filling, healthy food but in a self-serve style. I just bake up potatoes, shred a huge bowl of lettuce and put out small bowls and containers of whatever you would put on a salad or potato along with bottles of dressings and sauces. You can have anything you fancy, but here are some ideas for toppings:

For potatoes:

Sour cream

Butter

Chives

Cheese

Canned chili

Tomatoes

Broccoli

Cheese sauce

For salad:

Tomatoes

Canned kidney and/or garbanzo beans

Onions

Olives

Cucumbers

Sprouts

Cheese

Cabbage

Garbage Salad

Ingredients

Lettuce

Shredded carrots

Kidney beans

Tomatoes, chopped

Onions, chopped

Olives, chopped

Ground beef or turkey, cooked and cooled (optional)

Homemade ranch dressing with taco seasoning mixed in

Shredded cheddar cheese

Nacho Cheese Doritos (or Fritos Corn Chips, if you prefer)

Method

Shred a huge bowl of lettuce and add everything but the dressing and cheese until the very last moment. Crumble chips on top.

This was a friend's recipe, but I think many know this one. I turned it into a bit of a nacho salad. I love making the packets of ranch using whole fat buttermilk and mayo. Then I add packet taco seasoning to taste.

Punjabi Bean or Lentil Soup (Bali's recipe)

If you learn to make these sautés you can make all sorts of bean and lentil soups. You can also cook meats in these sautés.

Ingredients

1 pound of any kind of beans or lentils, dry

1 onion (red or yellow)

1 pepper (we use mild peppers)

3 or more cloves of garlic

1 ounce fresh ginger

2 tomatoes, chopped

1 cup fresh cilantro, chopped

1 tsp coriander seeds

1 tsp cumin seeds

1 tsp turmeric

1 Tbsp masala seasoning (There are masalas for beans and meats. They are small boxes of mixed seasonings you can find in the Indian foods section of the grocery store or at

Indian food stores. You can even find them on www.amazon.com.)

Oil

Salt and pepper to taste

Directions

In a large pot, add washed beans or lentils of choice.

Add water until there are two inches of water above the beans/lentils and begin to simmer on medium heat.

Add turmeric.

Chop up all the vegetables and add half an onion and one tomato to the soup in the beginning.

Add half a teaspoon of pepper and full teaspoon of salt, about a teaspoon of oil, and a few minced cloves of garlic.

In a skillet add a tablespoon of oil, coriander and cumin, and toast for a minute or two.

Next, add remaining garlic, onions, tomatoes, and peppers.

Sauté for about 2-3 minutes.

Add a heaping teaspoon of masala, then sauté and cook for a few more minutes, or until vegetables are soft.

Add cooked vegetable mixture to pot of cooked beans or lentils.

Add cilantro at the end.

Peanut Butter Cookies (source: www.myrecipes.com)

I love this recipe because it's cheap. I always have the ingredients on hand and it takes just minutes.

Ingredients

1 cup peanut butter

1 cup sugar

1 egg

1 tsp vanilla extract

(Nuts, raisins, and chocolate chips are all optional)

Directions

Mix all ingredients and spoon globs onto a cookie sheet, about two inches apart.

Bake for 10 to 15 minutes at 325 degrees Fahrenheit.

I always double the batch!

Easiest Cheesecake Ever

This is a no bake, super easy, and so good recipe. I have no idea where I got it from.

Ingredients

1 store bought graham cracker crust

8 oz cream cheese

1/3 cup sugar

2 tsp vanilla extract

1 cup sour cream

Directions

Use a beater to mix cream cheese, sugar, vanilla extract, and sour cream.

Pour into graham cracker pie crust.

Chill in fridge for at least 4 hours to allow it to set.

Homemade Sugar-Free Lemonade

Ingredients

Water

Lemons

Stevia (you can also use real sugar, honey, or maple syrup, but then it won't be sugar-free)

Method

In a pitcher filled with water, add as much squeezed lemon juice and Stevia as you like.

Keep adding sweetener and lemon juice until it tastes yummy.

Moon Beam Tea (source: *The Help Yourself Cookbook for Kids: 60 Easy Plant-Based Recipes Kids Can Make to Stay Healthy and Save the Earth* by Ruby Roth)

Ingredients

Hot water

Chamomile tea

Honey, agave, or sugar

Milk or plant milk

Method

Brew tea in hot water.

Add sweetener and milk of choice to taste.

The kids love this tea and I drink it at night.

Cranberry Water

Ingredients

Water

Cranberry juice

Ice

Method

Add 1 part cranberry juice to 3 parts water.

Serve over ice.

This is a great way to get kids to drink more water in the summer. I usually use pure cranberry juice without sugar and add Stevia to it.

Homemade Yogurt

Ingredients

1 gallon of milk

1 cup of yogurt (you can use some from your previous batch or buy at the store if you are just starting out)

Directions

Add milk to a large Dutch oven or any pot with a tight-fitting lid.

Simmer slowly until temperature reaches 200 degrees Fahrenheit.

Remove from heat and let cool to 115 degrees Fahrenheit.

Turn oven on to preheat for about 10 minutes.

In a separate bowl, combine 2 cups of heated milk with 1 cup of yogurt.

Whisk gently and add back to Dutch oven or pot and stir to combine.

Place in turned off oven and leave overnight.

If it doesn't firm up, let sit for a few more hours. The house and/or oven must be warm. This allows it to solidify with all the good bacteria and cultures. This is so healthy, and the cost is $1 for a big container instead of $5 or more for organic yogurt at the grocery store.

Vegan Chocolate Cake (this sounds funky, but it is better than regular cake)

Ingredients

2 ½ cups white flour

¾ cup to 1 cup cocoa

2 tsp salt

2 tsp baking soda

2 cups honey

1 cup coconut oil

1 cup water

1 cup almond milk or soy milk

2 tsp vanilla extract (you can substitute and use any other

preferred extract such as maple, coconut, etc.)

Directions

Preheat oven to 350 degrees Fahrenheit.

In a large bowl, mix together flour, cocoa, salt, and baking soda.

Add honey, coconut oil, water, milk, and vanilla extract.

Mix until combined.

Pour into a 9-inch cake pan and bake for 35 minutes, or until toothpick inserted in the center comes out clean.

Frosting

Ingredients

4 oz dark chocolate (you can use milk chocolate, but then it won't be vegan)

2 Tbsp coconut oil

1/3 cup water

Directions

In a medium saucepan, add chocolate, coconut oil, and water.

On low to medium heat, stir frequently until melted. Pour on top of cake.

Whole Wheat Pizza Crust

Ingredients

1 tsp sugar

1 ½ cups warm water

1 Tbsp active dry yeast

1 Tbsp olive oil

1 tsp salt

2 cups whole wheat flour

1 ½ cups white flour

Directions

In a large bowl, dissolve sugar in warm water.

Sprinkle yeast on top.

Let stand for 10 minutes.

Stir in olive oil, salt, whole wheat flour, and 1 cup of white flour.

Pour out onto clean, floured surface and knead in remaining white flour until dough becomes smooth.

Place in oiled bowl, lightly coating dough.

Cover with towel and let stand for 1 hour.

After 1 hour, your dough should be doubled. Place dough on floured surface and divide into two parts.

Form into tight balls and let rise for 45 more minutes.

Oil pizza pans. Roll out and stretch to fit pans and load with desired sauce and toppings.
I just use Hunt's tomato sauce with extra garlic powder and Italian seasoning as my sauce.

Bake at 425 degrees Fahrenheit for 14 to 20 minutes. Yummy.

Mom's Spaghetti Sauce (this was my mother's sauce from what I remember, with a few things added or taken out)

Ingredients

Hunt's cans of tomato sauce (very inexpensive)

Ground beef

Ground pork sausage

Green bell pepper, finely chopped

Italian seasoning

Freshly chopped garlic or granulated/powdered garlic

Directions

In a large pot, brown meat until fully cooked.

Add sauce, bell pepper, and seasonings.

Simmer on low heat for about an hour or so.

The longer it simmers on very low heat, the more flavorful the sauce. You can make your own tomato sauce, as well.

Homemade Tomato Sauce (This is from *Dump Dinners*, with some added ingredients)

Ingredients

Tomatoes (very ripe)

Onions

Salt

Butter

Italian seasoning

Garlic

Directions

In a large pot, simmer for one hour.

When cooled, blend and store in refrigerator.

Vegetarian Black Bean Enchiladas

This is my own little creation. This dish is so good!

Ingredients

Black beans, homemade or store-bought

White rice, cooked with chicken bouillon, preferably

Cheese (mild cheddar, jalapeno cheddar, or cotija)

Corn tortillas

Green enchilada sauce, canned

Butter

Directions

In a large skillet, heat up a stack of corn tortillas with a touch of butter, until they are soft and pliable. Set aside.

Grease a casserole pan.

Have all three cheeses shredded and mixed on a big plate.

Place tortillas side by side in pan.

Fill with beans and cheese and roll.

Arrange side by side.

When pan is full, sprinkle cheese and pour the can of enchilada sauce on top. Sprinkle more cheese.

Bake at 350 degrees Fahrenheit for 35 to 40 minutes.

Serve with white rice and beans on the side. You can use plain water or vegetable stock to cook the rice, if you prefer. Yahoo, it's good!

Frozen Bean and Cheese Burritos

Ingredients

Pinto or black beans, cooked

Rice, cooked

Cheese

Tortillas

Butter (optional)

Directions

In a big pot, mix desired amount of rice, beans, shredded

cheese, and any seasonings you like. Granulated garlic and onion work great here.

When everything is mixed well and cheese is melted, scoop into a large tortilla and fold to make burritos. Avoid overfilling.

Place all burritos seam side down on a greased cookie sheet.

Lightly brush tops with melted butter.

Bake at 350 degrees Fahrenheit for 20 to 25 minutes, or until golden brown.

Be sure to keep an eye on them so they don't burn.

Enjoy and freeze the rest.

These are delicious, much better than the store bought (because they actually have substantial amounts of beans and rice), and you can just take one or two out of the freezer and microwave to reheat. I make tons at a time.

Down-Home Chicken Soup

Ingredients

3-5 lbs bone-in chicken (whole, thighs, or legs)

Vegetables (all kinds)

Chicken bouillon

Italian seasoning or a combination of basil and oregano

Salt

½ lb egg noodles or pasta, cooked (rice or barley are fine, too)

Directions

Place chicken in a large pot.

Add water to cover.

Cook on low to medium heat for 1 ½ to 2 hours, or until internal temperature reaches 165 degrees Fahrenheit.

Once cool enough to handle, transfer chicken to platter to debone.

Return to pot, add bouillon, seasonings, and salt to taste.

Simmer for approximately 15-20 minutes more.

Add desired vegetables and continue to simmer until they are soft.

Add cooked egg noodles or pasta and serve.

You may use rice or barley instead. Pasta and rice get mushy in soup after some time. Egg noodles are the best for this soup. You can also just use chicken and vegetables and serve with some freshly baked bread.

Atta Flatbread

Ingredients

2 cups atta flour

1 cup water

3-4 Tbsp butter

This is what I call an Indian tortilla.

Directions

In a large bowl, add the flour and water and mix to form a dough.

Make into small balls.

On a floured surface, roll out each one.

Add a pat of butter (approximately ½ tablespoon) to hot pan.

Cook each flatbread for about 30-45 seconds per side. Serve warm.

Wheat and white atta flour can be found at Indian grocery stores, the international foods aisle at some grocery stores, and online. Buy a big bag and keep it on hand for these delicious flatbreads.

We eat this with everything. His curry chicken, my black beans.

Cheap and Easy Snack Ideas

Snacking is fun and can be nutritious, so I like to make healthy snack plates. Sometimes my kids and I just graze throughout the day and then eat a proper meal in the evening with Bali.

- Cheese and raisins
- Homemade raw granola bars made with oats, nuts, seeds, nut butters, and raisins (great recipes can be found online)
- Olives and pickles
- Organic yogurt loaded with probiotics (try plain Greek and add berries or make your own)
- Sliced and/or chopped fruit with nut butters
- Vegetables with peanut butter or hummus
- Seeds, nuts, and dried fruit
- Popcorn with coconut oil, nutritional yeast, and salt
- Homemade sliced bread with jam, nut butters, or cheese
- Sprouts
- Shredded carrots and red cabbage with a little ranch or dressing of your choice

- Salad (most kids actually like salad and if they say they don't, just keep serving it, trying different dressings, and they will eventually)

Make your own versions of frozen convenience foods. I make frozen lasagnas, frozen cheese, bean, and rice burritos, frozen enchiladas, and so much more. Just cook a double or triple batch of lasagna, soup, or casseroles, and freeze the extra.

Substitutions For Name Brand Convenience Foods (some of these recipes are from *The Complete Tightwad Gazette*)

Cocoa Mix

Ingredients

10 cups powdered milk

6 oz non-dairy creamer

1 lb Nestle Nesquik Chocolate Milk Powder

1/3 cup confectioners' sugar

Directions

Mix well. Store in airtight container in a cool, dry place.

Shake 'n Bake (remember this oldie, but goodie?)

Ingredients

4 cups flour

4 cups crushed saltine crackers

4 Tbsp salt

2 tsp onion powder

3 Tbsp paprika

Directions

Mix well. Store in airtight container in a cool, dry place.

Raisin Oatmeal Scones

Ingredients

1 ½ cups flour

1 cup dry oatmeal

1 tsp baking soda

½ tsp salt

¼ cup margarine

½ cup raisins

¾ cup sour milk (milk with 2 tsp vinegar)

1 egg, beaten

Directions

Preheat oven to 400 degrees Fahrenheit.

In a large bowl, mix flour, oatmeal, baking soda, salt, margarine, raisins, and sour milk until all ingredients are combined.

Roll out to approximately 3/4 inch thick, and cut into squares or shapes.

Place on large cookie sheet. Bake for 10 minutes.

Remove from oven, glaze with beaten egg, and bake for 5 more minutes, or until golden brown.

Seasoned Salt

Ingredients

8 Tbsp salt

3 Tbsp black pepper

2 Tbsp paprika

½ tsp onion powder

½ tsp garlic powder

Directions

Mix well. Store in airtight container in a cool, dry place.

Taco Seasoning

Ingredients

6 tsp chili powder

4 ½ tsp cumin

5 tsp paprika

3 tsp onion powder

2 ½ tsp garlic powder

¼ tsp cayenne pepper powder

Directions

Mix well. Store in airtight container in a cool, dry place.

Onion Soup Mix

Ingredients

¾ cup dried, minced onion

4 tsp onion powder

1/3 cup beef bouillon powder

¼ tsp ground celery seeds

¼ tsp sugar

Directions

Mix well. Store in airtight container in a cool, dry place.

Seasoned Rice Mix

Ingredients

3 cups uncooked rice

¼ cup dried parsley flakes

6 Tbsp chicken or beef bouillon powder

2 tsp onion powder

½ tsp garlic powder

½ tsp dried thyme

Directions

Mix well and store in airtight container in a cool, dry place.

Cook as you would normally cook rice.

Country Biscuit Mix

Ingredients

10 cups flour

⅓ cup baking powder

1 Tbsp salt

2 cups shortening

Directions

Using a food processor or pastry cutter, mix well to make sure shortening is evenly distributed.

Store in airtight container. Lasts 1 to 6 months at room temperature, during colder weather.

You may also refrigerate. Use it the same way you would use Bisquick.

Meatless Monday Casserole

Ingredients

3 cups vegetable broth

¾ cups uncooked lentils

½ cup uncooked brown rice

¾ cup onion, chopped

½ tsp sweet basil

¼ tsp oregano

¼ tsp thyme

¼ tsp garlic powder

1 ½ cups shredded cheese (use your favorite)

Directions

Add all ingredients (except cheese) to a baking dish and mix.

Cover and bake at 375 degrees Fahrenheit for approximately 1 ½ hours, stirring once halfway through the cooking time.

Sprinkle cheese and return to oven for an additional 10 minutes, or until it has melted and is golden and bubbly.

Remove from oven and let cool for another 10 minutes before serving.

YouTube Cooking Channels

growing much of their produce, she has amazing ways to make the food budget stretch and find free food without taking from those in need.

Jan Creson

This is a great one for those of you who love Dollar Tree shopping. She makes some pretty creative dishes with ingredients that were all purchased at Dollar Tree.

Chapter 5

Learning Frugality from the Professionals

Mary Hunt's story is an excellent one to motivate those of you who are in debt. With credit cards and a shopping addiction, she was a homemaker who put her family in debt over $100,000 over a span of 10 years. She woke up to this reality and worked hard to get her family out of debt. It took her 13 years of working all sorts of jobs and side jobs as well as mastering frugality. She writes books and has blogs and websites. You can find her on www.everydaycheapskate.com.

Amy Dacyczyn, author of *The Complete Tightwad Gazette,* is a household name to this day. She was a homemaker who raised a large family and bought a home with land on her husband's small military salary. She promoted extreme frugality and thrift. Dacyczyn strongly felt that learning to save and conserve would get your family farther than someone having an extra job or having both parents work outside the home.

Daisy Luther is a woman who struggled as a single mother of two children. As I've mentioned previously, I have recently been enjoying her books. I have *The Ultimate Guide To Frugal Living: Save Money, Plan Ahead, Pay Off Debt & Live Well; The Flat Broke Cookbook: Thrifty Meals and Shopping Tips for Tough Times; The Prepper's Canning Guide: Affordably Stockpile a Lifesaving Supply of Nutritious, Delicious, Shelf-Stable Foods;* and *Prepper's Pantry: Build a Nutritious Stockpile to Survive Blizzards, Blackouts, Hurricanes, Pandemics, Economic Collapse, Or Any Other Disasters.* I highly recommend them all.

We have gotten out of debt through our own experience, rebuilt lousy credit/no credit, purchased houses and land, and live comfortably on a small income. Off the top of my head, I would say your foundation will be growing as much of your food as you can, learning to preserve this food, getting into the habit of not spending or shopping, and developing creativity and outside the box thinking.

I truly believe that everyone can benefit from living a frugal lifestyle. You live without worrying about paying bills. You sleep well at night. You enjoy your days because you are not worrying about money. You do not need much money. You do not need much stuff or much house, or even much car. We need much, much less than we realize. In European and Asian countries, families live in tiny homes and bike or use public transportation. They live humble lives and work less. Their top priorities are their family and enjoying their lives.

I would rather live in a 600 sq. ft. house and have all the time to be with my children, write books, read fiction, and play with recipes than live in a big house and have to join the outside workforce, leaving my children in someone else's care while I work for a boss making him or her money.

Other people I learn from are those who make it on government assistance or one income. Connie Hultquist wrote the book *Dear Kitchen Saints: Letters From an Iowa Housewife*. She struggled to raise her children alone in a shabby house, while living on government assistance. She made things work until her wild husband returned from gallivanting about the lands. He ended up staying and finally focused on taking care of his family. He performed whatever jobs he could get, but they never struck it rich. They made it work on one blue-collar job. I enjoy her discussions of how she made hearty meals that stretch and how she and her girlfriends who were in similar situations made homes out of run-down houses. They even made their homes charming. They fed their children well. They never spoke of poverty. They just kept things running along with faith and creativity.

Mrs. Sharon White is a homemaker who chose to focus on her home while her husband provided for the family. I believe she talks about doing some side work, but ultimately, she feels that it is enough for a woman to focus on the home and let the breadwinner figure out how to provide. Her book *Living On His Income: Remembrances and Advice for the Christian Housewife* helped me a lot. She shares her mother's, grandmother's, aunt's, and mother-in-law's ways of homemaking. They were all content being at home and nesting. They took great pride in keeping things clean and tidy, taking care of what they had, having small flower gardens, and being busy. They did not run around town. Their husbands usually took the list off the fridge and did the grocery shopping when they had the chance. Family and church were the main social events in their lives. They loved being home.

In my videos and in a few of my books, I talk about an old friend I had, Miss B. I learned so many things from her. She made a paltry allowance stretch throughout the whole month. She struggled after a divorce and an injury that made it hard for her to work. Miss B raised two children on government assistance, and later she was diagnosed with an autoimmune disease and spent the last few years on disability. For years, she made things work for her children. She made holidays cheerful. They attended free festivals and parades with bottles of frozen water and homemade picnics in tow. When I would see her, we drank lots of homebrewed coffee, and her house was always spotless and cozy.

My husband and I are not struggling, but if we did not practice living well below our means, we might be. It is, however, a challenge until you grow accustomed to the simpler life. We do not go out to eat that much, and we don't go out to the movies. We do our hair and nails at home. We love going out and doing things, but we have been busy saving money to make a dream come true. Then the pandemic hit, which has made it quite easy to not do things because everything has shut down. It has been a very productive time at home.

In this modern time, it feels like a guilty pleasure to be at home. No commute, no working for The Man. But it is no easy task. You are running a household and nurturing a family. Even the dogs look to me for attention, exercise, and to run the house.

I think that just nesting, cooking from scratch most of the time (you get burnt out if you do it all the time), raising good human beings, walking pets, gardening, learning to preserve food, doing laundry, and cleaning the whole house frequently is a full-blown career or three. To feel that you must do more is not necessary. Some people make a career out of just housekeeping or being a nanny.

I did start a writing career and YouTube channel, but it is not for everyone. I also burned myself right out and had to reevaluate it all, downsizing my workload. I used to publish a book every three months, write a blog almost daily, and film for YouTube many times a week. I became very grumpy and even quit at one point.

Just know that all the money you save the family by working with the budget, finding sales, and decorating from thrift stores is enough. Scratch-cooking alone saves a fortune. Raising your children saves thousands in childcare costs. Not running around saves gas and wear and tear on the car. You do not have to pay a dog walker or a house cleaner. You do not buy tons of take-out and prepackaged foods that cost so much. You do not have to pay a gardener once a month to mow and trim the shrubs. You are also creating a home that is cozy and clean. Your family comes home to order and a hot meal. They get back to their sanctuary from this fast-paced and sometimes unstable world.

How I Work at Home

I do work. I do my homemaking and child-rearing, and I have two small hobbies that turned into careers. We pull in a small allotment of funds from my work, and for that, I'm so grateful. I have immersed myself in things I love to do, and now I make some cash to pay utilities or buy groceries. Yay!

"Choose a job you love, and you will never have to work a day in your life." -Confucius

We never had the extra money to build a shop or start a business. I love to write and talk. I love my life as a housewife and mother. I learned to write and publish books about this life. I learned to film our life. In the beginning I was awkward and rustic, to say the least, but I have learned and played with it all to put forth better work. It's still funky, but I have fun, and in the end, that is what matters. Having fun. Creating and building, but with the energy of playfulness.

I have used cheap laptops and free programs to publish books, and a very outdated cell phone to record my vlogs for YouTube. I have learned to edit videos and make book covers, all for free or little money. I'm not a professional, but I figure out what I need to without becoming consumed or taking time away from my family and life.

A woman in our YouTube community has a small cottage industry at home: baking bread for extra cash. Is this a future way of becoming a shopkeeper? In the days of old, a person's house was used for living *and* as a shop.

You can do many things right from home if you need to bring in extra money to get the bills paid. You can have garage sales or sell items on Craigslist or eBay. You can start a daycare. You can write books or blogs or start a YouTube channel. Those last two take a lot of time to develop and monetize, though. You could walk dogs and clean houses. The wonderful thing about these jobs is that they give you control of your schedule, so you can fit them in around your family's needs.

The Basics of Saving Your Household a Lot of Money

Through experience, I have learned that a kitchen garden can feed your family for months and save hundreds of dollars in the produce department, especially organic produce. Some of us cannot always afford organics, but we know it is best for our family's health. Suppose you can grow as much produce as you'd like, especially the expensive kind such as avocados, pomegranates, nectarines, and greens. You would be thrilled at how little you'd actually need to spend in the grocery store.

I have learned to stretch foods by using other less expensive foods. Keep cream of mushroom on hand to make cheap and easy casseroles and cream of corn on the shelf to make moist, heavy, and delicious cornbread.

Frozen vegetables are cheaper and sometimes more nutritious than fresh vegetables. Fresh vegetables travel far, while frozen are harvested and frozen immediately.

You all know my love of Dawn dish detergent. I continue to buy it despite its cost, because it's so useful. I use it to make many household cleaners, emergency laundry detergent and stain removers, for flea baths for my dogs, and I can water it down often since it is so condensed.

I have tried all sorts of stain removers with no luck. One summer I had a foster child, a girl who wore mostly pink and peach colored clothing and would play outside all day. Her clothes oftentimes had mud and berry juice on them. I kept a bar of Zote bar soap on the sink and, with some water, would lather it into the clothing and let sit overnight. Her clothing was always sparkling clean and stain free. As a bonus, it is unbelievably inexpensive. It will last for a year. My experience has been that it gets out all stains if treated immediately.

We eat very little meat. I am mostly vegan, and my family is primarily vegetarian. If we consume meat, we typically buy a whole roasted chicken as those are the very cheapest. It also saves on natural gas and seasonings, since it's already prepared and ready to eat.

The Less You Buy, The Less You Spend

You can live without paper towels and paper napkins. I rarely buy or use paper anything. When we have parties, I use our regular plates and utensils. I use mason jars for drinks. I use old clothes turned to rags for cleaning, and if a mess is very bad (having anything to do with dog poop or vomit, urine, or anything else that comes with all the joys of parenting dogs and children), I use the worst rags and throw them out when done. I use cloth napkins. I have a large pile in a basket at the table, and you can use them a couple of times before washing. I recommend going for dark colors if you decide to buy cloth napkins. I have a basketful of kitchen towels on top of the refrigerator as well that I use for all kitchen jobs.

If you know how to, crochet your own dish rags or use small washcloths. I love using both of these. You can wash them and reuse them a million times. Sponges begin to stink and hold bacteria after a few days or weeks.

Get a bagless vacuum. Have a steam mop or cloth mop that you can reuse.

Use menstrual cloth pads. I thought this would be disturbing because I rinse them out by hand before I throw them in the wash, but these are the best thing ever. The disposables are the ones that are gross. You see and smell the mess. The reusable pads I use have a gray wicking material, and you do not see, smell, or feel anything. You rinse under the tub faucet, and it is not bad. I have never had to worry about not having any menstrual supplies during the month.

Cloth diapers save $40 to $80 or more per month. If you are strapped for cash, there is nothing more stressful than trying to figure out if you have enough money for diapers and food to feed your children. Once you master washing them, cloth diapers are just as easy as disposable. I've noticed that WinCo and Walmart are now selling cloth diapers, so more people must be catching on.

You can buy seeds, fruit trees, plant starts, herb plants and such using food stamps. WinCo has seeds and plants. Walmart may have fruit trees. Dollar Tree sells seeds and garden tools for cheap.

Get a filtered water pitcher or filter for your kitchen faucet for cleaner, better tasting water. If you usually buy bottled water, this alone will save you thousands of dollars and you will be reducing plastic waste. I've heard that PUR is a good filter, but Brita removes chlorine. Berkey is a top of the line filter and cleans out everything from metals to prescription drug residue, but it costs $350 for the filters and canister, which in the long run is quite reasonable and worth it. The good news is that the filters last from six to 10 years.

Get yourself a handheld milk frother and small stovetop Italian espresso maker and learn to make your lattes and mochas at home. It will cost you $1 per drink at home as opposed to $4 at the café. You can even throw in an extra shot of espresso at no cost.

Get a Roku box or cheap Roku TV at Walmart or Target. You will easily replace your $100 monthly cable bill with a massive list of free channels and music. If you *must* have HBO or Disney Plus, you can add it for a few dollars per month.

I have a radio that I bought for only $1 at the thrift store. It sits on my kitchen cabinet, and I get all the fantastic local stations.

Bathe and walk your dog. Clean your own house. Many people pay for all of this. When you have the money, it is great. I take my dogs in to get their nails trimmed and my little dog's glands drained. When we are flush with cash, I get them bathed and brushed well. Mostly we do it ourselves, except for nails; I am terrified to do their nails.

Learn to really, truly do laundry. Separate it, get stains out, iron, mend. This preserves your wardrobe. I stick to jeans, yoga pants in dark colors, t-shirts in dark colors, and plaids. I know how we are, and these clothes last the longest and show less stains. I especially love jeans for the boys because they are so durable.

If you love cream in your coffee, try buying a gallon of milk instead. Whole milk, of course. It is much cheaper than all the small containers of creamer, and has less fat and calories, lasts longer, and goes farther. You can have a latte every single day.

Shopping Spree on a Budget

Once a year, we will travel to a Savers thrift store in the bay area. It is where the wealthy live and donate all their quality goods and clothes. This store is huge, clean, and organized. I try to wait for a 50% off sale. We will take a few hundred dollars and drive the extra hour and a half to shop for everything. I will stock up on at least two to three years' worth of clothing for the boys. I buy for all seasons and events: daytime, nighttime, play clothes, nicer clothes for special events, school co-op days, outdoor gear, jackets, pajamas, and hats! I will even splurge on new or used toys, games, and puzzles. Just about everything except for shoes is purchased second-hand. Then I stock up on linens, towels, kitchen tools, baskets, candles (if priced low), rugs, and whatever else we want and need.

The last time we did this was almost three years ago, and we spent $500. However, I have not had to buy the boys anything except shoes, underwear, rain boots, and mittens. I stocked up my family's closets for the next three years. I bought stacks of towels and sheets that are still in good condition. The boys played with the used toys for two years, and then we gave them to other children. I love to simmer tea in my big, floral teapot while listening to my little $2 radio sitting atop my kitchen hutch—both from Savers.

Decorating on a Budget

Christmas is over, and New Year's Eve has passed. What did not get taken down and packed away were the twinkly lights. I find them enchanting. Home Depot has crazy sales on holiday lights and goods right after Christmas. We stocked up, and our house was decorated with twinkle fever. We have warm strands of twinkle lights, icicle lights, and colorful twinkle lights throughout the house. It has cozied up the place.

Our house is dark, especially in the winter. So, when we gazed upon our Christmas tree in glee, I realized that what I love most about the holiday season is the glimmer from festive lights inside the house and outside on people's porches. Why keep it to one month a year? Why not have the cheer year-round?

Your home is *your* home. It is for *you* to choose its colors and sweetness--not the magazines, not your family, and not your friends. Oh yes, they all have suggestions, and they know how your house should look. But do not cave. Do not decorate according to this season's top picks or what is popular. Why do you think Victorian and vintage stuff is so popular? It has charm, character. It is outdated now by decades, maybe centuries, but people still desire these things. They are classic.

So, nothing is outdated or out of style. You find what you love deep in your heart. If you love pastels, do it! If you love hardcore purples, do it! Find furnishings and colors that make you smile when you walk through your rooms.

When we moved into this house, I did not smile when I walked from room to room. The walls were white, but it did not brighten up the home like I thought it would. It gave it a weird glow. The floors had gaps that the boys' Legos and dog hair got into. The furniture that looked cozy in the other house now seemed so big and awkward. I began to plan and strategize.

I have told a long story in my blogs, videos, and last book, so I will not bore you, but I found "other" furniture. I cleaned the house of most of the old furniture. The only pieces that survived the significant change were the beds, dining room furniture, and a few paintings. I purged with a fever, then hunted for free or moderately priced replacements. I did not care if they were in fashion or not. I wanted things that fit this funky little house with its tiny square rooms. I also needed more shelves for all my books, candles, plants, and photos.

My curtains do not match, but they are long and warm. I have hauled them from house to house since the first time I bought them to keep the warmth in and the cold out. I love my kitchen table. I put the extra leaf in it to make it bigger. We use it to play board games, eat great food, write, drink coffee, and hang out. I knead bread dough and stir things on this table. My children do schoolwork on this table. Neighbors and friends have sat at this table and played cards, talked about life, made confessions, and laughed with us. My husband and I have made more plans for the future at this table.

I have a simple cover for my overstuffed chair since it was gently used and then kept in a dusty garage. It has a floral print on white fabric, and the dirt shows easily on it, so I bought a chair cover in an antique blue shade for $25. It already has a hole in it, but it is a minor thing to be expected with boys and dogs in the house. I spent lots of time curled up on that chair, typing away. I am typing from my worn-out throne right this moment.

The couch is a tan pillow top that my husband calls "the magic couch" because he falls asleep every time he stretches out on it. It was $125 and unused, found on Craigslist. It usually goes for over $500 new.

I have stained glass art hanging in my windows and colored glass baubles catching the light. My kitchen is busy with jars full of ingredients filling the glass door cupboards. I have big shelves that we tore out of the water closet and kept for my kitchen. I recently painted it barn red with a jar of paint that a neighbor gave me.

The house and porch were all tan when we bought the house. I dragged out the five gallons of blue paint left over from our old house, and we painted the railing a happy blue. We hung birdhouses, chimes, hummingbird feeders, and stained-glass art off the eaves of our porch. The yard is filled with bird baths, bird feeders, a large garden, flowers, and fruit trees galore.

I dream of my yard becoming a wild jungle filled with fruit, vines, cornfields, and flower beds. Perhaps even a hammock and some point, where I can sip lemonade made with ripe, fresh lemons from my tree (that is, if it survives this new mountain climate).

Chapter 6

If You Are Super Poor

It might sound like we do not do hardcore living at all. But that is the trick and the truth about mastering frugality and thrift. It becomes a challenge to look forward to because, with each victory, you will find yourself enjoying it more. If you live frugally for years, it adds up, and after some time, you do not even notice.

You will notice how paying bills becomes so easy that you do not think about it. You pay them. You sleep well at night and look forward to the day. You do not notice much having to do with money, and you do not think about money much because the struggle is gone. The worry is not there anymore. The paycheck covers all the month's expenses and keeps the pantry full.

I used to pray for wealth. When I struggled to pay my bills, the debt was overwhelming, and car payments still haunted me monthly. I do not think that way anymore. Now that we have no debt or car payments, there is a savings for when an emergency arises, bills and mortgages are paid with ease, and we even have a little money to play with. We do not need as much as we think we do.

My husband and I still have two mortgages, which is not considered frugal at all. However, both mortgages are small. The rental property pays for itself with a profit of a few hundred dollars. The mortgage amount for the house we reside in is precisely the amount of rent we used to pay back in the days when rent was affordable. It is the same amount as the small apartments near us. Either way, we have to pay a mortgage or rent. This way, we own the house, the payment is affordable, and we know a landlord will never raise our rent.

We have installed solar panels at both homes. Fruit and nut trees and kitchen gardens fill both properties. Our tenants enjoy low rent, small electric bills, and plenty of free, organic food.

We enjoy low electric bills, a low mortgage, a profit from the rental, and every year we will harvest more and more free, organic food.

This year I have created a "hardcore" frugal plan to pay down one mortgage quickly. That is the only goal, but it is significant. We got a deal on this house, but we live in one of the most expensive, overtaxed states. We now live in a genuinely lovely area where the average house costs $400,000 and up. Our home was $233,000.

So, what to do? We have land, and I know that it will serve us well if we use it wisely. We grow tons of organic food and save thousands of dollars a year. We make our property lovely and lush, and our home cozy and sweet. That way, we love being home and do not have a desire to travel, at least for now. If times were difficult, we could raise hens and rabbits, ducks, and even a goat. We have land to grow food in order to thrive.

We only have a quarter acre, but it is significant, and I have learned that you do not need more than that. Watch The Dervaes Family on *Urban Homestead*: https://www.youtube.com/watch?v=7IbODJiEM5A&t=379s&ab_channel=UrbanHomestead

This family resides 15 minutes from downtown Los Angeles, California. In a 4,300 sq. ft. yard, they grow enough food to feed themselves and sell to local restaurants to bring in an income. They have goats, ducks, and chickens as well.

Land is the one most important thing to look at when buying a house, not how pretty the place is, although it should have good bones. But if you have enough yard and decent soil to grow food, you are on the right path.

When it comes to a house, you can truly clean up and fix up almost anything. We have fixed up our homes inexpensively with fresh paint, some help from a handyman, and lots of scrubbing. We've torn out carpets and oiled old floors back to life. We've covered damaged old floors with new flooring material purchased at a huge discount.

We have lived in several small homes and shared small bedrooms while saving and planning for our own home. The boys have always shared a bedroom and always will. I honestly believe they will have a stronger bond because of it. In other countries, families live in tiny homes. They are shocked at our giant houses, huge minivans, and even our colossal food portions. We are a super-sized nation.

I've said it before and I'll say it again. We rarely eat out and we rarely shop online. A big treat for us is when I make homemade treats such as ginger snaps using a recipe from *Allrecipes.com*. Sometimes Bali brings me a real chocolate bar (Milky Way is my favorite). If we have soda, it is considered a rare treat for special occasions. We may get a fountain soda when we are on a road trip.

We used to be much looser when it came to treats and snacks from the store, but since we gave up palm oil, we have had to make everything from scratch. Now we also do it to save money. Homemade cookies are less toxic than store-bought Oreos (although I do love those too).

You can make all your cakes, cookies, and candy. In *The Complete Tightwad Gazette* by Amy Dacyczyn there is a recipe for candy. I think it's Jim's recipe. I tried it once without success, but I will be trying it again since it sounds delicious.

I've read and reread *The Complete Tightwad Gazette* and other frugal books. They keep me motivated and learning. I recently joined The Tightwad Gazette Facebook fan page in order to find my people.

I always think back and assess where we could have done things for free with some patience and creativity. I still play what my friend and I call the "What If We Were Super Poor?" game. It may sound odd, but it helps to teach us frugality on Olympic levels and prepares us for challenges.

For example: one night, our tenants called to inform us that the central heating and cooling system went out. I knew this day would come as the system was old and ready to go. I'd had it repaired twice when we lived in the house, and each time, I was told it was on its way out and given an estimate of $10,000 to replace it. I was prepared.

We got a few estimates, and sure enough, the companies wanted $6,000 to $10,000, and that wasn't even for the complete job. We did not have that kind of money saved, nor did we want to spend that amount. I remembered my trusty "What If...?" game and we found heating and cooling window units. We read the reviews, purchased three units including four-year warranties on all three, and installed them ourselves. Our tenants now have a much better, more efficient system than the old ceiling vents that never really got the house warm *or* cool. It cost us a total of $1,700.

What if you cannot afford to put in a garden? All you need is a $10 shovel and to wait until winter with lots of rain to soften the soil. Do a no-dig garden and layer it with cardboard, paper, leaves, grass trimmings, horse manure (scratch the waste if you do not have a way to pick it up), and compost from your kitchen scraps. Read *Farm City: The Education of an Urban Farmer* by Novella Carpenter.

As mentioned before, you can get seeds from the dollar store or with food stamps. You can get fruit trees from Walmart. Learn how to propagate. You trim a good branch from a fruit or nut tree, cut off the stems and leaves so it is just a stick, put it in a potato (yes, you read that right), and put it in the ground. Do more research on YouTube. I learned this from Ron Finley (The Gangsta Gardener): https://www.youtube.com/watch?v=7t-NbF77ceM&ab_channel=UPROXX

I found him when I subscribed to www.masterclass.com. You could start a whole orchard from other people's trees. It would take years to bear fruit, but it would be free.

What if you cannot afford the laundromat, or your washer breaks down, and you don't have the money to fix it? Use the sink, tub, or a bucket and buy some Foca or Roma powdered detergent. It is the cheapest out there, smells great, and cleans laundry well. Azalea on *Way Crunchy* (YouTube) used to hand wash all their clothes in the tub when her washer broke. She was newly divorced, in a whole other economic bracket, and money was limited. She filled her house with used furniture, grew a garden, and hand washed everything. Her link: https://www.youtube.com/channel/UCR2eVqOK1dHzXJpUr00PA3A

What if your vacuum breaks? Hopefully, you do not have wall to wall carpet. If so, you will have to borrow a vacuum between sweepings. Maybe find a cheap hand push carpet cleaner like they have at restaurants. I have a vacuum but have taken to sweeping my entire house.

My house is filled with free furniture. I do not often turn away hand-me-downs. I will drag things off the street. I even pull over shamelessly if I see an item on the road, and I will bring it home. I scour, bleach, and wash it back to goodness. If someone offers me a bag of clothes, I accept it thankfully, and then I sift through it. I keep the good and give the rest away.

You never have to purchase a book, movie, or magazine. You can find anything for free online or at the library, even music!

If you have no money to stock your pantry, find food banks, get on food stamps, and even consider dumpster diving. *Freaking Frugal* has a channel on YouTube, and that is what they do to save money. They are ordinary people; the woman is amusing. Here is the link:https://www.youtube.com/channel/UCR4u4zBm37-uODgDlvsu7Bg

If you feel you are not in that much need and do not want to take food from the food bank, do what *Homestead Tessie* on YouTube does. She goes at the end of the week or month when her local food bank is throwing away food that is still good. She takes it before it hits the dumpster, but then she feels like she is not taking it from others in need. Most of the food is particularly good, and she preserves it to extend its life. She will either can or dehydrate produce before it spoils, or repackage flour, nuts, milk, and much more. Here is her link (search for her food bank videos): https://www.youtube.com/channel/UCqJgpaYNmI2UksYZ_fmK6jw

What if you are too poor for a car? Try to live near work and schools, libraries, grocery stores, and clinics. You can walk farther than you think, and you will be in shape! You can also bike to many places.

What if you are too poor for your rent or mortgage? Downsize. That is all I can say. Downsize like your life depends on it and find cheap housing. Kids can share rooms, and you and your hubby can sleep on pull-out couches. *Frugal Jo* has a great story about that here: https://www.youtube.com/watch?v=y4jAlQF9reI&ab_channel=FrugalJo

She and her family had a lovely big house to go along with cars and yes, lots of debt. They wound up downsizing to a one bedroom flat in a bad neighborhood. They did this for a few years in order to recover financially. It's a good story; I recommend checking it out.

Downsize and make the extreme cuts now before things get too hard and before you and your family become homeless. Swallow your pride. Work whatever job you can get, live where you can afford it, eat rice, beans, and potatoes.

And the last but most crucial part. What if you do not have your health? Poor health is common these days. People are struggling with health issues. Most times, things can be turned around, and almost 100% prevented with proper nutrition and exercise. Eat healthy and pack in the nutrition in every meal. Even if you cannot afford organic foods, familiarize yourself with the Clean Fifteen list and choose whole grains, whole wheat, and brown rice. Eat mostly vegetarian, loading up on vegetables and fruit. Wash your produce well using water and white vinegar. Exercise daily and vigorously for physical and mental well-being. Exercise is free. Walk, jog, do yoga, Pilates, and weights.

You can find workouts on YouTube or walk and jog in parks and on trails.

Don't drink or do drugs. Drug and alcohol abuse is common today. Seventy percent or more of the population is estimated to be addicted to drugs and/or alcohol. Do everything you can to get sober and stay sober if you are part of that population. When I read the book *Evicted: Poverty and Profit in the American City* by Matthew Desmond, the two most significant issues that stood out were poor choices and addiction. The roots go much deeper, but addiction will destroy a person, their life, and their family's life. Drug and alcohol addiction often lead to violence, depression, poor choices, poverty, and homelessness.

Do all you can to learn to be mentally calm and positive. Try not to follow the news. Spend time in nature, listen to music, play, and find your hobbies and joys. Your mental health is of utmost importance.

Hard times are a cycle. They do not have to last; they can be a season or two. It can all be temporary.

Learn everything you can about this lifestyle, and you will find a new freedom and joy. I promise. You will build a beautiful life. You all will thrive and not just survive.

Visit me on my channel:
https://www.youtube.com/channel/UCLvRv0K42rVxYY9Cj8bJiWg

Email me: vondola@yahoo.com

Facebook (very new as I have stayed off of social media for years): https://www.facebook.com/kate.singh.359/

Kate Singh

Pro Home Cooks

As mentioned previously, this used to be *Brothers Green Eats* but the brothers have gone their separate ways. The older brother, Mike took over the channel. He is so talented. All the old videos are still on there and they are very fun to watch and learn from. You can learn how to make everything, and I mean EVERYTHING: Japanese, Chinese takeout, bagels, sourdough, Indian street sandwiches, sauces, kombuchas, simple food for work lunches, budget meals, fancy dishes, and on and on. You can even learn about canning! **This is my favorite channel.**

You Enjoy Life

This is the younger brother, Josh's new channel. This is a great one for healthy and super affordable meals.

Simply Sara Kitchen

I love her older recipes and have tried many. They are always easy and fantastic. Her vegan corn dogs, minestrone soup, mushroom stroganoff, crab rangoons, and buckeye balls are repeats for sure.

Homestead Tessie

Tessie and her husband live in a fixed up mobile home on one acre of land that they have turned into a farm, complete with gardens and chickens. In addition to